Heaven Came to Me

Heaven Came to Me

GOD REVEALED THROUGH COMPELLING AND CONVINCING TRUE STORIES

Marlene Sommer

New York

Heaven Came to Me
GOD REVEALED THROUGH COMPELLING AND CONVINCING TRUE STORIES

Published in New York, New York, by Morgan James Publishing. Morgan James and The Entrepreneurial Publisher are trademarks of Morgan James, LLC. www.MorganJamesPublishing.com

The Morgan James Speakers Group can bring authors to your live event. For more information or to book an event visit The Morgan James Speakers Group at www.TheMorganJamesSpeakersGroup.com.

Shelfie

A **free** eBook edition is available with the purchase of this print book.

CLEARLY PRINT YOUR NAME ABOVE IN UPPER CASE

Instructions to claim your free eBook edition:
1. Download the Shelfie app for Android or iOS
2. Write your name in **UPPER CASE** above
3. Use the Shelfie app to submit a photo
4. Download your eBook to any device

ISBN 978-1-63047-565-9 paperback
ISBN 978-1-63047-566-6 eBook
Library of Congress Control Number:
2015902159

Cover Design by:
Ryan Rhoades

Interior Design by:
Bonnie Bushman

In an effort to support local communities and raise awareness and funds, Morgan James Publishing donates a percentage of all book sales for the life of each book to Habitat for Humanity Peninsula and Greater Williamsburg

Get involved today, visit
www.MorganJamesBuilds.com

Habitat for Humanity®
Peninsula and
Greater Williamsburg
Building Partner

Contents

Preface

I did not visit Heaven. Heaven came to me. I have been incredibly blessed to have God reveal Himself to me personally, in both many worldly and spiritual ways. Whether I have been suffering through a personal loss or comforting a friend, truly improbable circumstances combining at just the right moments have convinced me of God's presence and love in the most difficult times. These many true astonishing life experiences have reinvigorated and reaffirmed my faith in God. There is a God. God shows His presence in quiet and reticent manners or in gallant and glorious ways. The many miraculous moments I have experienced were definitely more providential than circumstantial.

I am not a person who spends time in Bible study. My husband and I have an active social life. We hang out with our close-knit neighbors for a driveway party, meet our fun group of friends at someone's house to drink a few beers and watch the O.S.U. Buckeyes, or go boating on Grand Lake. And I love to travel and shop with my daughter and my sisters!

I am just an ordinary, everyday person who has been touched by the extraordinary. My amazing lessons have taught me how to endure many real struggles and heartbreaking experiences that have ultimately brought me to a personal relationship with God. These experiences have enabled me to relate to and empathize with others and to encourage them to fight through their own hardships and sorrows in life. I hope readers will relate to me because I am not a minister or a celebrity, but, rather, just a typical small town wife, mother, Girl Scout leader, school board member, friend, neighbor, and co-worker from Ohio.

Never in a million years would I have believed I would be writing anything about God. I have drawers full of children's books that I have written for the past twenty-five years, and my goal was to pursue publication when my own children were grown. It is beyond my wildest dreams that, instead, I would have these incredible life experiences to share about God. In fact, it is weirder for me to be writing about my own life than it would be for my favorite NBA star to pursue a second career as a jockey! I can just see my favorite super-sized Cleveland Cavalier player mounted on his horse, with his long, dangling legs dragging in the dust, as the announcer delivers the thrilling drama of the exciting finish… "It's

Basketball is Overrated… it's Basketball is Overrated in the lead…Basketball is Overrated is coming into the stretch… Basketball is Overrated WINS the Derby!" Definitely a long shot, and so am I. Yes, I never would have dreamed I would be telling readers how Heaven Came to Me!

In fact, I went from bunny dip to genuflect in my life plans. For my high school graduation gift, my aunt and uncle took me on a very nice trip. We traveled north through Michigan and the Upper Peninsula and south through Wisconsin, with our last stop at The Playboy Club Hotel in Lake Geneva, Wisconsin. It was an absolutely huge and beautiful resort nestled among rolling hills and serene lakes. Inside the resort, I was so impressed that the bathroom stalls were as large as a complete bathroom in a house, each having its own phone! When my uncle took me out to the discotheque one evening, I was so mesmerized by the glamour of the Playboy Bunnies that I thought I wanted to be one. I should have known that such a silly fantasy would not be God's plan for my life. I only had to reminisce back to the summer after my sixth-grade year.

One afternoon at the local swimming pool, a boy in my class said, "Kessler, you are a carpenter's dream! Yeah, you are a carpenter's dream!"

With an inflated ego, I strutted around the pool in my little bikini, showing off my deep, dark tan and flipping my sixties, waist-length hair back off my shoulders.

As I walked by the boys again, one guy repeated, "Yeah, Kessler, you are a carpenter's dream alright…flat as a board!"

My self esteem instantly deflated like an inner tube and went right down the drain of that swimming pool!

Up until only a few years ago, I never would have believed God's plan for my life would be to write about the incredible circumstances that have brought me to this point in my life. I guess being a Playboy Bunny was definitely not my calling, but then, none of us ever knows what God has planned for our lives.

I suppose God decided to use me to share my experiences because I am very loquacious and outgoing. He must have looked and me and said, "Hmmm, I have not given her any talents, but boy can that girl talk! I will use her to tell a world that has forgotten about Me that I am still here for everyone."

I started talking in full sentences when I was eighteen-months old and haven't stopped since. When I was in kindergarten, my teacher moved me and my little friend, Michelle Millisor, to take our naps on top of the tables because we could not be quiet.

At my parochial school, we had to go to confession routinely, and I always confessed the same sins.

"Bless me Father for I have sinned. I talked in church and fought with my sisters." (I might throw an impure thought in just to spice it up.)

As soon as I got back to my pew, I was elbowing my friend kneeling next to me and already talking again before I even said my penance.

"What did you get?" I implored.

"Three Our Fathers, three Hail Marys, and three Glory Bes," she replied.

"Yep, me too!" I giggled back.

In high school our German teacher, Sister Wilhelmina, would put her finger to her lips with a "Shhh… Bitte… Fraulein

Kessler… Nein!" as she shook her head from side to side. But as soon as she turned her back, my friends and I were talking about guys and planning our outfits for the weekend.

And nothing kills a romantic moment like asking your husband, "Did you remember to take out the garbage?"

I always joke that I could talk non-stop on a three-thousand-mile, cross-country road trip with my good friend Vicki Laux.

God must have realized He created someone who can't shut up, and, so, He might as well use my mouth to spread His word. God touched me personally with extraordinary experiences because He must have known my extroverted personality would eventually agree to tell others that He is always there for each of us. My multitude of unique life experiences has been too incredible for me to deny sharing with others.

Let's face it. We don't all have an angel appear and ask us to be the mother of God. Only one special person received that honor. Would you have faced being an unmarried teenage girl with the risk of being stoned to death? Mary was brave and said, "Yes!"

We all have the opportunity, however, to be God-like or angelic in our actions. Every one of us is afforded that possibility. We can choose to say "Yes!" to God every single day of our lives by doing the good works He expects of us.

Still, we often do not heed His voice.

Matthew 25:35 'For I was hungry and you gave me food, I was thirsty and you gave me drink. I was a stranger and you welcomed me, naked and you clothed me. I was ill and you comforted me, in prison and you came to visit me.' Then the just will ask him: 'Lord, when did we see you hungry and feed you or see you thirsty and give you drink? When did we welcome you away from home or clothe you in your nakedness? When did we visit you when you were ill or in prison?' The king will answer them: 'I assure you, as often as you did it for one of my least brothers, you did it for me.'

When I did what God asked me to do and began sharing my experiences of God revealing Himself to me, I was taking an enormous step out of my box. I have to admit I was a little embarrassed until I realized that there was no reason to be embarrassed when serving God. It was such a big deal, though! I really felt as out of character as Evan in the movie "Evan Almighty"! My many "signs" were just as crazy to me as Evan's were to him.

There were times when I was often a lazy Catholic who would rather go shopping at Macy's than attend Mass on Sunday. If I gave an hour of time to church each week, I reasoned that I was doing enough. When I was a teen, my classmates thought students in Youth for Christ were "Jesus freaks," and, admittedly, I could never imagine outwardly expressing my faith as they did. How embarrassing that might be. Now I am giving talks on faith, sharing my experiences with God, and doing spots on Radio Maria?

I am sure when my friends have been out socializing over a few beers, they have possibly gossiped about me and whispered, "What the hell's up with her?"

Somehow I didn't care. Why me? I do not know. There are countless people better than I. For example, I could not compare to my own mother's capacity for goodness. And, yet, she never had any experiences like mine (other than the experience you will read about in chapter seven). Millions of people throughout time have believed that the miracles told in the Bible truly happened. We all love to hear about miracles from the past. We also long to hear about miracles in today's world. There is no reason why God would not want to give us miracles today because the world is definitely in one heck of a mess. He wants to let His presence be known in every way He can.

I knew I was called to share my experiences. Sometimes, without thinking too much about it, I just forged ahead. The concrete signs God sent my way were too magnificent to ignore. When you hear that voice of the Holy Spirit, you know it is God. It can seem unrelenting and nagging, still and quiet, or as loud as a bullhorn, even though it is not actually audible. Even if you don't understand what you are feeling, you clearly know that you cannot say no. Opus Dei teaches that everyone is called to holiness and an ordinary life is a path to sanctity. Make your ordinary life extraordinary!

I did speak with numerous priests, all of whom were totally supportive and encouraging. They definitely believed God was calling me, and still I hesitated. But that strong support of many people and friends ultimately fortified me with the courage I needed. I could plainly see how God worked through me and those around me. My advice is never to deny the voice of the Holy Spirit that is leading you. You may feel as if you are in the dark many times, but God will always bring you into the light. He will always lead you to fulfill the destiny He has planned for you. I am now fulfilling my obligation to tell how Heaven came to me. I am sure you can recount times when Heaven came to you.

Chapter 1

Jesus Came from Heaven

I looked Evil in the eye when I was five. Evil. Satan. The Devil. The little red guy with horns and a pitchfork. Call him what you will, but let it be terrifying! As I grew older, I preferred to call him Son of a Bitch.

I also met God on that same day. God the Father. Jesus Christ. The Holy Spirit. The kind and loving Jew with the beard and the long hair. Call him what you will, but let it be glorifying! As I grew older, I preferred to call him Son of God.

I learned early on that one represents evil, lust, hatred, and greed. The other is goodness, purity, love, and generosity. I chose to be friends with the good guy.

Many children's earliest memory may be their first day of kindergarten or a trip to Disneyland. I wish my earliest memory was a pleasant one, but it is an experience of profound trauma.

The day I met Evil, I was a five-year-old child on a play date with a new little friend. I also met a minister that day. Yes, he was a man ordained to draw others closer to God. But, he was possessed by wickedness. I went to this minister's home as an innocent child to play with a new friend, but I left with a trauma that would terrorize me for many years of my life.

I somehow found myself standing in an upstairs bedroom with this depraved man, my lace trimmed silk panties at my ankles.

"I'm going to brand you!" The words uttered from the reverend's lips would be forever stamped in my mind. I never forgot that moment. It would live on every day of my childhood and stay with me forever. I never went back to that house again.

I did not know or understand what happened in the bedroom that day, but I knew it was disturbing and wrong. I blocked out most of that painful experience. Evil can possess anyone and anything in this world. Even a minister who is supposed to live and preach God's love can be overtaken by vile, immoral forces.

It was not a priest who was my predator, even though I was a little Catholic girl. All of the priests I knew were wonderful, gentle, and kind men. The Catholic Church was definitely not the only faith that was tainted with pedophiles. The degeneracy that exploited my innocence can often masquerade as something pure and good.

Some nights, if it was late, my loving father often stood one of his four little daughters in the bathroom sink and bathed her arms, legs, and feet with a warm, soapy washcloth after a long day of play instead of giving all of us a full tub bath. My feet were probably always dirty because I loved to go barefoot. That evening, my father stood me in the bathroom sink to wash my legs and feet.

On that particular night, I pointed and told my dad that my "tinkler" hurt. (That was a term a polite little girl in 1960 might call her private part. You went "potty" or "tinkle." Never would we use a crass and impolite term that is common today like "pee" or "poop.") My dad dipped his index and middle fingers in a jar of Vaseline and gently soothed the salve over the red and sore skin of his third little daughter's private area. He told me that the soreness must have resulted from riding my bicycle or sitting on the cold sidewalk while playing hopscotch.

God showed His heavenly care that day through my loving earthly father, who nurtured and rescued me from the painful memory of my dreadful experience. I learned early on that God often shows His love for us through the efforts of others.

I would not have known how to tell my dad what had happened to me because I did not know myself. We didn't know anything about the "birds and the bees," let alone sexual abuse, because we had not been exposed to that evil, nor had we been told of its existence. The period in which I grew up truly was a time of innocence.

I grew up in a loving, nurturing family that was not dysfunctional. This tragedy, unfortunately, can happen in the best and worst of family circumstances, and I am sure my parents never dreamed that something so horrible could happen to one of their children. Although it was very distressing to me, I really could not fathom what had happened to me either. I blocked out everything except the memory of standing with my panties on the floor and his telling me he was "going to brand" me.

I later understood that it is not normal for a pre-pubescent child who does not even have peach fuzz, let alone pubic hair or shaven legs, to encounter her first sexual experience. For most girls, sex first occurred with a hormone-raged teenage boy in the back seat of a car or, ideally, as a bride wearing sexy lingerie in a romantic honeymoon suite. Neither of those scenarios applied to me, a five-year-old child who still wore lacy-trimmed, little girl panties and cotton, bow-trimmed undershirts.

In about fourth-grade, I remember asking my mother how babies were born. I thought your belly button opened up and the baby came out. When she revealed the shocking truth, I was incredulous!

I crossed my legs and said, "Don't tell, Kathy!"

I wanted to spare my sweet sister from this dreadful news!

I remember when my own daughter was a student at Immaculate Conception Elementary School. She was soon going to be educated on sexuality through the "Growing and Changing" series of books.

One night when I put her to bed, she timidly shared, "Mom, Courtney said… Courtney said…when you have a baby…the man puts his penis in a woman's vagina!"

Taking a deep breath, I launched into this important parent-child conversation. In the most matter-of-fact voice I could muster, I said, "Yes, honey, that is how you have a baby."

She flew up from her bed, horrified by this startling revelation!

"Oh, my God! You and dad did that three times!"

After calming her down, we had a nice talk, and I finally settled her down to go to sleep.

Unexpectedly, she lunged up from a reclining position again, "Grandma did that five times!"

She was inconsolable. I prayed that she would remember that same repulsion through her teen years! Our family still laughs at her innocent reaction to this fact of life. My child's response to intimacy validates that God's gift is fully intended for adults.

Because of what I had endured, I was so paranoid about anyone molesting my children that I would often role play when I gave them a bath. I would say, "Don't ever let anyone touch your private parts, even if it was Father ___ or Mister___ or anyone else." I would mention one of my favorite priests or friends, who I knew would never do such an awful act, in order to make a point.

"You say, 'No!' and you run and tell me!"

"Even if someone said they would kill your mom or dad, you must tell me. Don't believe them; they are trying to frighten you. We will always take care of you and keep you safe."

Years later when I watched the movie "A Time to Kill," I realized what a blessing it was that my father never knew my secret because he may have been like the father in that movie, who went after the men who abused his daughter. My dad idolized his four girls, and if anyone had ever harmed one of his precious daughters, especially in the way the minister traumatized me, he might have taken the law into his own hands.

My father was a star athlete in high school who earned eight varsity letters in basketball and football. He was scouted by Ohio State and Notre Dame for football and played on a pro basketball team when he was young. A survivor of the Depression, he later served in WWII as a sharpshooter in Nazi Germany, where a general shook his hand for his precise, long range marksmanship. In short, my father was a brave and strong man. If I had told him what had happened to me, I could imagine his taking a baseball bat, flying out the screen door, and storming over to that "son of a bitch," beating him to a pulp. He might have killed the man with a baseball bat or his bare hands! It is frightening to think what might have happened.

It was important that I didn't share my abuse with Dad. This disclosure would have ruined his life because he never would have gotten over the heartbreak and pain of what had happened to his innocent daughter. Therefore, it was meant to be that this would be my secret to carry for decades. I am so glad I spared my dad that emotional pain and torment through the strength that God gave me as a little child. Actually, it took me many years into adulthood to divulge my humiliating secret to my mother, with whom I had always shared absolutely everything.

My father adored all four of his daughters and was always there for us. We were his number one priority at all times. He was a dad who proudly took all four of his little girls in our organza dresses, hats, and little white gloves out for orange juice after Mass on Sunday. It took remarkable patience for my father to get forty tiny fingers into four pairs of gloves! He took us on car rides for ice cream almost nightly in the summer, and he always produced white, waxed-paper bags of powdered sugar donuts and maple-frosted sweet rolls from the bakery on the kitchen table every Saturday morning for us to eat while we watched cartoons. The donuts were almost a daily treat in the summer. Holidays, too, were extraordinarily magical and memorable. Clearly, my dad spoiled his girls rotten.

My dad usually took my sisters and me upstairs to bed and stayed until we fell asleep. I will never forget his own original stories about the adventures of "Pepper and Dondi." The twosome was a little black dog named Pepper and a young boy named Dondi. Generally, they were going on a trip or adventure somewhere. They always ate my favorite food, which was steak and corn on the cob "swimming in butter," and usually they were on their way to California. I routinely fell asleep before they arrived at their destination of Disneyland. I cherished my dad's stories and adored him all the more for reciting them to me over and over. His unconditional love and kindness proved to me that all men were not bad.

That minister would visit me every single night of my childhood in my dreams. Every night of my childhood, for years and years, I had nightmares of that house.

He would come in the form of a wolf every night in the same recurring nightmare. I would be running home from that house, chased by a big black wolf. The wolf stood on two feet like a man, and he would be rapidly chasing me as I was trying to run as fast as I could to get away from him. Despite my frantic effort to go faster, I would run in slow motion, like Chico Marx in the old-time movies. I would run and run, my little heart racing and pounding, trying to escape my predator. He seemed always at my heels, attempting to grab me while I was dashing to get home. In each replay of this nightmare, my little legs would always carry me to safety in my yard.

The back of our property was lined with a border of raspberry bushes separated by a white gate. I would hurriedly swing the gate open with a tremendous sigh of relief. Running between the bushes and quickly closing the gate behind me, I would be so happy each time to have reached safety, like Dorothy coming home from Oz.

I could not stop yet, though. I would continue running by the red and black raspberry bushes, and then by the cherry, apple, peach and pear trees. I would pass by the fragrant rose bushes and all the varieties of beautiful flowers and our huge garden of fresh organic vegetables. At last, I would reach my big, white, two-story home and fling the back screen door open, finding the comfort I desperately needed. My heart would still be pounding in my chest, but I would be back where love abounded.

Each and every night, in the darkness of my bedroom, when I lay my head on my pillow to go to sleep, the desperation and nightmares would always come again.

But, when the sun came up in the morning, I felt indescribable happiness because the love of my parents and my sisters would come shining through, just like the rays of sunshine on my pillow.

Every morning my mother would call upstairs, "Good Morning, Glory!"

I would rouse from sleep, my little pink, bowed-trimmed, cotton undershirt wet with perspiration from my nightmare, to the sound of my mother's melodic voice ringing up the stairs. Joyfully, I could escape the terror of my sleep to the love of my mother, father, my three sisters, and my grandparents who also lived with us. My grandparents proved to be a tremendous blessing in my life, offering their love, faith, knowledge, and affection daily.

The smell of my grandmother's homemade yeast cinnamon rolls, smothered in creamy vanilla icing, would waft up the stairs, and I would be back to where I belonged. My nightmare was forgotten as the love of my family permeated my life for the day. But, as darkness came and I went to sleep, the wolf would visit me again and again. I would not enjoy peaceful slumber for all of my childhood years. The wolf chasing and my heart racing would be my nightly ritual.

My dreams were not the only reminder of my childhood trauma. It would haunt me at different times in my life and pop up in many circumstances.

I never knew what the word "brand" meant as a young child. But, that powerful word that was given as an order to me would be stuck in my mind forever. When I went to the movies years later, I shockingly learned the real meaning. I was sitting cozily in my red velvet seat, eating buttery popcorn out of the original red and white-striped, cardboard box and cradling a lapful of candy. My eyes were intently fixated on watching the western on the big screen. Suddenly, a cowboy took a sizzling, red-hot iron and seared the animal's buttocks to "brand" a steer. My jaw dropped and my eyes popped as I imagined being seared with a red-hot iron burning my skin and "branding" me for life. It was like wearing a scarlet letter!

I felt so sick and weak that I probably dropped the box of popcorn. Its contents were likely scattered on the floor, to be trampled on by movie-goers leaving the theater. I have forever hated that word and have sensed a chill anytime I have heard it spoken throughout my entire life.

I met Evil the day my innocence was stolen from me but I also met Jesus. Jesus came to me as a child. We had a picture of the Child Jesus hanging in our hallway at the top of the stairs. It was not of the dark-skinned, dark-haired Jewish child that the Son of God became. Instead, it was an image of a blonde Christ Child that looked much like my sisters or the children of our Caucasian German community.

Jesus came to me as one child to another. He rescued me from Evil. He was like a best friend to me. I stood before Him, and it was as if God Himself was telling me everything was alright. I was going to be fine. I would see Him and then go off and enjoy my day, knowing He was always there for me. Even though I was blessed with a large loving family, I learned early on that, even when you think you have no one, God is always there for you, to see you through every obstacle. You can be isolated on a deserted island or in the midst of a massive, shoulder-to-shoulder crowd in Times Square, and God is right there with you. You can be in an utterly miserable, hopeless situation, and God is right there with you, ready to answer your needs in the blink of an eye.

Under the image in the picture at the top of the stairs were the words, "You I seek. You I mean. You, Yes You, I love you!"

All during my childhood (and sometimes even in the troubled times of my teen years), I would stand before this picture, staring into the face of the young Son of God and repeat the words that were written below it from one child to another. I would read those consoling words over and over, sometimes tens of times a day.

After my daily visits with the Christ Child, I would run off happily to play and enjoy my day, like someone getting a morning coffee with a jolt of caffeine. This was like a true hug or kiss from Heaven to start my day.

It was as if God revealed Himself to me personally that day. I stared into the eyes of Jesus, as a child like me, coming to me, comforting me, and giving His love to me. I would feel a special union with Him and His love. I was the most important person in the world to Him. (The truth is that everyone IS the most important person in the world to God.)

God's love for me would erase the terrible thing that happened to me. He would lift me above that awful moment so that I could live a happy life. I was an ordinary little five-year-old child in the middle of the farmlands of Ohio who needed someone to help me escape my horrific experience. God knew right where to find me! He had no difficulty spotting me in the beautiful Land of the Cross-Tipped Churches, encircled by miles of abundant cornfields. Little did I know what an extraordinary and healing experience I was receiving! God would reveal Himself to me many more times in my life.

Often, God comes to us through other people. In my case, He used my father to rescue me by tending to my physical and emotional wounds. We all have the opportunity to have God's love shine forth through us to others every day by exhibiting acts of kindness and compassion.

"Who do you think you are? God?" people sometimes remark to a person who appears to be a know-it-all.

"Yes, maybe I do!" I suppose someone could answer.

We can all feel God working through us. His role is bigger than that of the President of the United States, a movie star, celebrity athlete, or a Fortune 100 company president. We are not kids playing dress-up. We truly mirror God when we allow the Holy Spirit to work through us with love, compassion, and benevolence to those who intersect our lives. Each of us has the capacity to embody the power of the Holy Spirit working in us and through us. As we tap into this gift, we will gain the ability to serve God in an exponential way, guaranteeing incredible happiness in this life and in eternity. Viewers love watching Ellen DeGeneres make people happy through the acts of kindheartedness and philanthropy she promotes on her T.V. show. God loves watching all of His people make others happy through our own acts of kindness and generosity.

Most of my early life when I made the sign of the cross, I would slowly pronounce in the name of the Father, and of the Son, and then hurriedly slur…and Huh Sprrr…Amen. The Holy Spirit was the forgotten one, like I sometimes felt as the third child of the family. It took me about forty years to realize that He was one powerful force! I guess I am really a slow learner when it comes to certain things. Mr. Bill Sacher, my high school geometry teacher, could certainly agree with that assessment.

Thus, I am telling you, nobody, not even that Evil, Satan, Son of a Bitch, could steal my joy in life. So, every morning and before bed at night, I would look at the picture of the little blonde Christ Child and repeat the words that were ingrained in my mind, body, and spirit…"You I seek. You I mean. You. Yes You. I love you!"

My life was happy and full of love because of God and my wonderful parents, grandparents, sisters, neighbors, and friends. God's love was shining through all of these people to me throughout my life. Later on in life, my husband and children would show God's love in the most magnificent ways ever.

Years later, when we were moving my mother from the big, white two-story house on Anthony Street, where we grew up, to a smaller ranch house, I found that special picture of Jesus among the hundreds of items that three generations accumulated in our large home. I brought it to my own home and tucked it away with other treasures so I would always have my special reminder of one way God connected to show His intimate and personal love for me. By that time in my life, I did not need to see His face to feel His presence. I found Him anywhere and everywhere. He had become my constant companion, that personal assistant. He helped and guided me in every situation. I saw His face in many people.

As I grew older, I often forgot about Him and went about my life as if I didn't need God anymore. I left Him for periods of time, sometimes for years, much in the way a teenager disengages with his parents until he realizes their importance in his life. I thought I could be independent from God, too, but I could not. I went running back to Him so many times in my life.

Because God has come to my rescue many times in my life I have come to realize how much He values every person's life. I have gained so much insight into how God helps all of us and developed a greater appreciation of God's presence in everyone's life. God is revealed through every race, religion, and culture. It does not matter whether we are Christian, Jew, Muslim, Hindu, or Buddhist. God may be called by a different name and worshipped in a different manner, but He transcends all the differences. He loves all of us the same. He created each one of us in His own image. His creation is therefore represented in a variety of racial and ethnic backgrounds, nationalities, family configurations, sexual orientations, abilities, and religious traditions. (The last sentence in this paragraph, which expresses my feelings precisely, was written by the remarkable parishioners at St. John's Norwood, Chevy Chase, MD., and used with permission from Rev. Sari Ateek.)

Every single human throughout time was created by our one miraculous God and loved intensely and equally. Therefore, God wants each of us to love others intensely and equally, regardless of our differences. To please God, we simply have to love one another and be kind to one another. We will, in turn, love God. This is not such a big demand at all; it is very easy and benefits everyone. Wouldn't it be wonderful if everyone in the world would embrace this philosophy?

I shared my trauma many years later with my sister, a therapist, and my mother, mainly because I wanted to know more about the family that lived in that house. While I had blocked out much of it, I still remembered many details. Understandably, I never told anyone else about this incident.

When I did confide in my husband decades later, he was totally supportive. I felt so blessed that our marriage was never affected by my tragic incident. We had a normal, healthy, fun, and sexy relationship. Nothing could threaten our relationship because my husband and I shared a true and deep love that was rooted in the sacrament of marriage. God did indeed bless me by healing me from my physical and emotional wounds. He blessed me by giving me an amazing husband with whom to share my life. God was at work again. He has worked overtime a lot in my life!

Several times in my life during great times of stress, the nightmares also came back. When my dad was dying, I was fixating on a sex criminal in the news and his horrible abuse to his victims. Extremely sensitive to cases like these, I found myself identifying with the victims. My terrible flashbacks and dreams revisited me. I have never been able to read or hear about sexual abuse incidents without feeling personally impacted. I don't even like to watch horror movies or thrillers where any human being or animal is hurt in any way. Nevertheless, despite a few apprehensive moments along the way, God's love completely healed me from my abusive incident. Through His help, I have had a happy and mentally healthy life.

It was not until my own daughter, a psychology and sociology major in college, heard my story that I truly accepted it was not my own fault. I had been going through a great deal of stress with my youngest sister battling breast cancer. The nightmares started coming back.

One particular weekend, my daughter came home to be with her beloved aunt who was fighting breast cancer. With my being so stressed at that time, I told her about what had happened to me as a child.

"Don't ever tell anyone," I begged her.

"I would be so ashamed. People would look at me differently," I stammered with apprehension.

It seemed to me that something like that could never happen to someone in a perfect loving family like mine. Unfortunately, sexual abuse can and does happen to countless families. What is important to remember is that the victims are not at fault and should not therefore, allow themselves to be defined as somehow dysfunctional because of what they have suffered.

"What!" my daughter exclaimed.

"How could you even dream that anything like this could ever be a child's fault? An innocent child of four or five who goes to play at a new friend's house and becomes the victim of a terrible person? What if that happened to your child!" she raged.

Consumed by a mixture of anger and a need for retribution, she grabbed a phone and immediately started making calls to the minister's religious affiliation, hoping to track down the person. No, I did not want to pursue this person! I did not want anyone to know! Why should I seek revenge? I would not sue or take money from a religious organization. It was not their fault! This monstrous pedophile, whom I did not even know, would not ruin my life.

Later, I discovered that the man had died, and I hoped he had found help and sought God's forgiveness before he passed. When we forgive someone, it frees us from the hurt inflicted upon us. I spoke with his religious affiliation and was informed that he had been moved around and was assigned supernumerary status. Eventually, he left or was forced from his church altogether.

I had a wonderful family whose support ultimately helped to free me from the memory of my childhood horror. After all, why should a child who suffers psychologically and emotionally from the injury to her soul not heal in the same way that a child who is stabbed in the arm is healed from a physical injury?

When I heard about another child sexual abuse victim in the news, and her torturous experience, I knew that she also came from a wonderful, loving family and had no control over what had happened to her, just as I could not control what had happened to me. She inspired so many by sharing her story. Indeed, her faith in God healed her, as my own faith had rescued me. Still, God's healing was not yet complete.

When I was a child, my First Communion meant a beautiful white dress and veil, a big party with a very special, decorated cake, and presents and money. The money was the best part! This sacred event was a rite of passage in second grade. Evidently, I thought I, not Christ, was the guest of honor! I did not know the accurate meaning of the Eucharist being the true Body and Blood of Jesus Christ. It took me many years into adulthood to come to the understanding of that actual miracle.

My sisters and I used to play "Holy Communion" in our formal living room as children. We would flatten white bread and cut out circles with a round, metal, tea-ball, kitchen utensil. Then, we would place the hosts into a beautiful, lead crystal candy dish that had a long stem and looked like a chalice. Emulating our elder Catholics, we would kneel down and stick out our tongue as the "priest" (one of my sisters) said "Body of Christ." Between the hosts and peanut butter sandwiches, we consumed enormous quantities of Wonder Bread as children!

When I told my mother almost fifty years later that someday I would like that lovely crystal piece that we played with as children, she told me that it was a gift from the minister's wife many years ago before they moved. Oh, my gosh! I was shocked that I never knew that! I was overwhelmed that the beautiful crystal piece that shone with light and prisms, the object that young girls played with to simulate Holy Communion, had been an article from that house where evil traumatized me.

Today, that stunning, cut crystal piece is displayed in my living room, and I enjoy the sparkling light shining forth from it daily. It does not bring back bad memories at all, only beauty and light. God's goodness triumphed in the end.

When asked about why children suffer, Pope Francis replied that he could not explain with words.

"Certain realities in life can only be seen through eyes cleansed by tears," he said. "I invite each one of you here to ask yourself, 'Have I learned to weep and cry when I see a child cast aside, when I see someone with a drug problem, when I see someone who has suffered abuse?'"

God certainly sheds a tear for every innocent child who is harmed, and He never forgets our pain. If He knows the number of hairs on our heads, surely He holds a special place for us in His heart and in Heaven. Because innocent children are very precious to Him, He does not make bad things happen to them. God never wills evil. I continue to feel so blessed that Jesus came to me as a child. Indeed, Heaven came to me.

Chapter 2

The Ascension into Heaven

*A*t my daughter's fourth birthday party, I noticed that my mother-in-law was not eating any food or snacks. She declined when I offered some hors d'oeuvres and mentioned she was having a few digestive problems.

Months later when she went in for gallbladder surgery, the surgeon came out with a very somber look as he explained to the children that their mother had a rare gallbladder cancer and would only have six to eight weeks to live. What a tremendous blow! Our lives took a complete turn in a moment's notice. One can only imagine how hard that news hit my wonderful mother-in-law and how it totally devastated her children.

Once the reality of her unfortunate diagnosis set in, she was the ultimate model of class and grace, despite her terrible plight. Always still a mother, she continued to be strong, uncomplaining, and loving. Amazingly, her wit and sense of humor followed her to the end.

Eight years earlier, her husband Andy had also died from cancer within two months of his diagnosis. He never knew, as any of us ever do, that his life would be taken so soon. But, this situation was dramatically different because such a grave pronouncement from the doctor was totally unexpected.

In hopeful desperation, three of the Sommer daughters and I traveled the dirt roads of Indiana to bring Sally to visit the famed Amish healer, Solomon Wickey. While he may not have healed her, he did offer her a sense of reassurance through his faith. As a result, she was much calmer and more accepting of her grave illness. Ultimately, the family exhausted all options of alternative treatment and lovingly resolved to make their mother's time left as comfortable as possible.

Sally's house became a bee hive of activity, with her kids and their spouses and grandchildren coming and going around the clock. Her son Dale's wife, registered nurse Nancy Heckler Sommer, took a leave of absence despite the threat of losing her job, to care for her mother-in-law. I will never forget witnessing the constant loving care and compassion she so tenderly exhibited to Sally. Watching Nancy was like seeing Mother Teresa herself at work. She never left the house for the entire seven weeks that she cared for her mother-in-law. (Nancy passed away from cancer at only forty-two years of age. Dale later married Paulette Miller, whose husband, also named Dale, died from cancer just three days apart from Nancy.)

With Nancy as the trained caregiver, she instructed the siblings on how to give palliative care during their beloved mother's last weeks. I was so impressed with the love and patience exhibited by all six of her children. Every single one met the challenge. Their example was a testimony to what their parents had taught them. Her daughters Patty, Jane, and Linda and sons, Dale and Tom, performed numerous acts of loving care and kindness for their mother. The daughters-in-law, Nancy and Julie, cared for Sally as if she were their own mother. My husband Steve sometimes slept on the floor at night beside his mother, feeding her ice chips and assisting Nancy. Sally's sons-in-law, Doug, Bob, and Ritch gratefully stepped in to support their beloved mother-in-law.

To this day, I still regret that I did not do more, even though I was pregnant and extremely ill. Still, I cared for our two young children so my husband could be where he needed to be every moment possible. Through it all, I learned, first-hand, life lessons about the power of love and compassion that would never be forgotten. God was once again working His will through others.

It was like a revolving door at Sally's household. Friends stopped, priests came, and lots of delicious food was delivered to the family. Eventually, there was a daily anticipation that scrumptious culinary delights would be dropped off by friends and neighbors. We found that homemade apple pie can indeed lift a spirit even a little bit in hard times. As we endured the most tearful moments of our lives, we also embraced those moments of extreme laughter that ironically come, even in the midst of deeply emotional family crises.

Many inexplicable "signs from God" happened throughout Sally's illness and after her death. After a while, the family would hum the "Doo... doo... doo... doo..." tune a la "The Twilight Zone" because of the occurrence of so many bizarre moments. There was the Easter lily that kept leaning toward wherever Sally was resting, and there was the night she died when all of the girls awoke, unbeknownst to each other, to the strong smell of Ciara perfume, their mother's signature scent. What I am about to share next will forever live on in my mind. On the particular morning of April 19th, all of the kids and their spouses were kneeling around both sides and at the foot of their mother's bed. Robert Mills, a close friend and honorary member of our family, was leading the rosary in a powerful voice. As Bob led and announced, "The Second Glorious Mystery, the Ascension into Heaven," Sally suddenly started gasping for her last breath.

My sister-in-law Jane, who was kneeling beside me, grasped my hand firmly and startlingly and tearfully gasped, "Oh my, God!" as she watched her mother leave this earth at the precise moment "the Ascension into Heaven" was proclaimed with Bob's precise enunciation.

With barely a pause, the family held hands and pulled together to recite the next four decades of the rosary. What a send off! Their mother could have died anytime during those seven weeks, and at any moment, but she did not. In the presence of her loving family, she passed on at the precise moment those words were said, not a moment sooner or a moment later.

As you read on, you will understand why God gave her family a sign that this wonderful wife and mother had "a straight shot to Heaven." On the surface, she may have seemed to be an ordinary, everyday person, but in God's eyes, she clearly was anything but ordinary.

My mother-in-law was polite and quiet, intelligent, hardworking, uncomplaining, honest, and genuinely good. Although she held down a big job at home, while her husband worked second shift at Ford Motor Company in Lima, Ohio, raising six kids was a lot of work and expense. The kids didn't have expensive clothes, but they wore clothes that were nice and stylish, clean, and always impeccably ironed. Inexpensive meals like cabbage soup and bean soup stretched the dollar and remain family favorites today.

Sally also had a great sense of humor and fun-loving side. Indeed, some of the best times in my life were spent going out with my in-laws and their friends. A twenty-something and a fifty-something sure can have fun together! Age does not matter in life. We could have a few drinks together at a bar or a Saturday night dance, and laugh until we cried into the wee hours of the morning. Yet their faith was always an example, and you still never missed Mass on a Sunday morning!

As a tribute to the person she was, all six of her children are also great individuals. The Sommer siblings are products of the outstanding qualities of their parents, and therefore I am blessed with the most amazing and fun in-laws in the world. They possess a strong work ethic because, even as children, they pitched in at home - mowing the lawn, shoveling the snow, cleaning the cars, and washing the dishes. Moreover, they were happy kids, totally unspoiled. In fact, on their birthday, it was special enough just to have everyone sing "Happy Birthday" and enjoy cake. No extravagant presents like our spoiled children of today expect. Only once did my husband receive the gift of a watch for a birthday present. Yet, he never felt that he was not unconditionally loved by two of the best parents in the world.

None of the kids is divorced, has ever been on drugs, or spent time in jail. They are professionals, business owners, and awesome mothers and fathers. In rural Ohio, they would be called "salt of the earth" good people. I never said they weren't ornery however. We continually laugh at family gatherings as we hash over childhood stories about the glowing statue Dale scared his sisters with coming down the bedroom hallway or the stink bomb he made in the garage, etc. etc. Invariably, many stories revolve around Dale's antics.

My mother-in-law gifted me with a husband who is the most hard-working, moral, and honest person I have ever known. He has such firm integrity that I swear he would walk a mile to return a quarter. He can always be counted on to do the right thing. He totally "gets" what is important in life.

As a bonus, I thought Steve was (is) Brad Pitt hot! I fell in love with him the summer after our eighth-grade year. He revealed the bluest eyes I had ever seen, and he sported the most gorgeous muscular legs and chest. I was head over heels! "Steve is so handsome!" is a remark that I have heard repeatedly throughout my life. This compliment was conveyed to me via my daughter's sorority sisters or even swooning ladies in their eighties. My dear friend, Margaret Mestemaker, the wife of a retired colonel in the Air Force, gushed about how handsome Steve was every single time I saw her.

How my mother-in-law ever raised a son like Steve is amazing because growing up, the boys only did the "man chores," like lawn mowing, car washing, etc. Now, though, Steve cooks, does the grocery shopping, cleans the house and bathrooms, does laundry, irons, and routinely prepares a delicious meal that is ready when I arrive home from work everyday. Even more incredibly, he owns his own optical business that he manages from our home. Extremely intelligent and practical, he can fix anything around the house. I think that God gave me this "calling" to share my experiences, not because of me or my talents, but because He knew that a man of Steve's character would always stand beside me to advise me to do the right thing.

Steve could not have been a better parent from the "get go," as he took on the responsibility of changing the diapers, giving the baths, playing and reading for hours every day with the kids, helping with homework, and coaching their ball teams. He even worked with our daughter on learning the splits for cheerleading tryouts! Steve once received the "Knight of the Year" award at a Knights of Columbus banquet, but he has always been "The Husband and Father of the Year" to me. In some of his finest moments, Steve helped take care of my one-hundred-and-one-year-old grandfather before he died (Grandpa only wanted Steve to help him to the bathroom), assisted my sister throughout her five-year illness with breast cancer, and served dinner to my eighty-seven-year-old mother almost every night. He even asked Mom to live with us in her old age. I can only thank his parents for the person that he is, and I am blessed to have kids who are just like him.

My in-laws are also blessed to marry a child of Andy and Sally Sommer because they, too, possess the same morals and ethics. Likewise, my nieces and nephews are remarkable individuals and great parents. I believe my mother-in-law's life deserves to be celebrated because she was a devout Christian mother who raised such an awesome family. Her entrance into Heaven was to be known and revered by her family as their words "the Ascension into Heaven" were recited in the faith they were lovingly taught.

Please believe that these coincidences are planned by God to happen at a precise moment and know they are messages from Heaven. God revealed that Sally, our special mother, was indeed in Heaven, where she is destined to live forever.

Millions of people appear to be just "ordinary" people. Nevertheless, I am sure many of you have these "ordinary," but truly "extraordinary" people in your lives as well. Think of them fondly and remember the impact they have had in your own life. One need not be written about in the history books or famous in this life to be acknowledged by God.

Chapter 3

The Hug from Heaven

As you have been reading, I have been blessed with many remarkably coincidental as well as physical "signs from Heaven" in my lifetime. I realize that my revelations are not necessarily unique. God has revealed himself to people throughout time. Because we have learned lessons from miraculous instances that have happened throughout history, why would we think God would not show His much needed presence in today's world? My own personal miracle has previously only been shared with family and several close friends. I suppose that I have worried that sharing what happened to me would cause others to think that I am some kind of kook. But, after years of prodding, I am finally going share a very profound event in my life.

Being a mother has, by far, been the most rewarding and wonderful experience of my life. I was blessed to have two children who were a constant source of pride and enjoyment. Like all mothers, I thought they were (and still are) the most beautiful and intelligent kids in the world! I loved my kids so much that I constantly felt overwhelmed with happiness, like a volcano ready to erupt with joy! When I became pregnant again, I could not have been any more excited to have a third child.

Unfortunately, this blessing came at the same heartbreaking time that my mother-in-law was also dying of cancer. I have come to realize that life is often a mixture of wonderful and terrible things happening simultaneously and that we have to find and savor all the joy we can from the good times. In this overwhelmingly sad and stressful time, I wanted my husband, Steve, to spend as much time as possible with his mother. Responding to her needs, he spent every day caring for her and often sleeping on the floor next to her bedside. After her diagnosis, Steve's mom was told she had six to eight weeks to live.

About a month after she died, we decided to go ahead with the dream Disney trip that we had been planning for quite some time, even though I had been very sick since I became pregnant. Ironically, I was especially surprised that I had become pregnant in the first place because, when my mother-in-law was dying, I hardly spent any time with my husband. Nevertheless, I did not question my good fortune, remarkable as it may have been.

We decided to take my mother along on the vacation, which ended up being a wise decision, since I was struggling with the pregnancy. The sixteen-hour drive to Florida was exceedingly difficult for me. Enduring the extreme nausea was almost intolerable and made for a miserable ride. Throughout the drive, my mother provided so much support by entertaining the children on this long pre-iPad ride. She also consoled me, holding my hand when I could hardly bear the discomfort any longer.

When we arrived at the Polynesian Village in Disney World I could barely walk. I almost collapsed because I felt unbelievably ill. Understanding my plight, the concierge moved us to a private office and offered refreshments as we awaited our room. By the time we reached our room, I was torn between seeking medical help and wanting to enjoy the trip of a lifetime with my family.

Ordinarily, I can will myself to keep going, no matter what the circumstances, but I was just feeling so incredibly ill. Something seemed profoundly wrong. I decided to try to rest for a bit and insisted that Steve and my mother take the children out for a while to discover all of the exciting possibilities offered by the resort.

The staff of the hotel was very concerned for my well being and looked after me by checking in every half hour to see how I was doing. Additionally, the staff showered me with lovely gifts: a plush Mickey Mouse, gourmet jams and jellies, a tin of Polynesian Village note cards, and other thoughtful mementos. They wanted to call an ambulance and tried to persuade me to go to the hospital, even offering transportation. However, I did not want to ruin our trip and said I really wanted to stick it out. Steve accepted all responsibility for the kids, and my mother devoted herself to my care. I was so sick that I seriously felt as if I might die.

The second day I felt a little better and was determined not to ruin this incredible trip for my family. Defying record heat and ignoring my own miserable state, we went to each of the parks all day the entire week. I did enjoy watching my kids, but, unfortunately, this was not the once-in-a-lifetime Disney vacation I had envisioned.

One day in particular, I was standing in line for the Enchanted Tiki Birds in the 100-plus temperature and had to squat because I felt so awful.

Other vacationers in the queue voiced concern and I simply stated, "I am so sorry. I am pregnant and not feeling well."

I was beyond caring about embarrassment.

Mercifully, after a jam-packed week at Disney, we returned home and settled back into everyday life. I soon had an appointment with my obstetrician and was relieved that I appeared to be okay, although I started spotting a little later that day. I called my doctor, who reassured me that everything was fine. Sensing no further problem, I stayed home with our four-year-old daughter, Alyssa, and insisted that Steve go on to coach our son Andy's baseball team with our friend, Kevin Riesen.

Later that evening, I did not feel well at all. When I went to the bathroom, I started to hemorrhage severely. All I saw was blood, lots of blood. I called for Alyssa to come help Mommy and asked her to get me a magazine so that I could fan myself because I was feeling so weak. When I left the bathroom and started walking toward the kitchen, I started feeling extremely faint and asked her to bring me the phone. I just remember everything fading and then feeling my body go completely weak as I collapsed to the floor. Alyssa called 911.

Steve came home before the ambulance arrived, and paramedics started to administer first aid. One of my best friends, Karen Riesen (Steve had called her to take the kids), literally fell into the house as she tripped while frantically rushing through the door from the garage to the family room. Our neighbors stood in their driveways watching the paramedics carry me out on the stretcher to the flashing red lights of the waiting ambulance. It seemed to take forever to insert an IV, using a tourniquet, before they rushed me to the hospital.

I was extremely concerned and repeatedly kept asking, "Is my baby alright?"

I will be forever grateful to paramedic Bob Schulte, a friend and former classmate, who continually offered his kind reassurance as the ambulance sped me to emergency care.

A typical woman, I was slightly concerned about the condition of my lingerie, after this bloody episode, when I arrived at the hospital emergency room.

Inside the ER, the doctor immediately started examining me and ordered an ultrasound. Since this was a small town hospital in 1990, there was no technician to administer the ultrasound. The staff put me in an examination room on a tilt table, my body practically upside down, while we waited for an ultrasound technician to come from Lima, a city about forty-five minutes away. It was the longest wait of my life.

When the ultrasound was being administered, I kept worriedly asking, "Is my baby O.K.?" Of course, the technician would not answer.

Finally, they moved me back to the ER, and the doctor came in to deliver the devastating news. Gravely, he stated, "I am so sorry, Mrs. Sommer. Your baby died."

Suddenly, I felt all the life go out of me. It was almost as if I were breathing my last breath. Understanding my distress, the nurses compassionately moved me up to the third floor, rather than the maternity floor, into a private room. I cried the entire night in that hospital bed. I will always remember the many acts of kindness of Sherrie Keighley, a very nice and most concerned nurse, who came and checked on me every hour.

The next morning, my doctor came in to examine me and said he had reviewed the ultrasound and now thought the baby was just sleeping! What! My world had ended, and now there was hope? Oh my God, my baby is alive! They were sending me home, where I was to watch for bleeding and come back to the hospital immediately if any blood appeared.

That night was one of the hottest nights of the year, and our house did not have central air. In spite of the heat, I was glad to be home with my kids and prayed for my baby to survive. My son's room was cooler than our bedroom, so I slept in his bed while Steve took the children to our room. The next morning I went to the bathroom and was very distressed that there was more blood. I was once again overwhelmed with apprehension.

We rushed back to the hospital, which was about ten miles away. After examination and testing, the doctor confirmed that our baby had died. We could wait to deliver, which might take hours or days, but he recommended doing a procedure to take the baby immediately. My husband thought it would be easier not to go into labor for an unknown period of time and cause more pain and misery. Already in a state of shock and grief, I agreed to my obstetrician's recommendation of the D&E, which to me was basically the same as a more clinical term for an abortion.

After the final termination of the life that had been sheltered within me, I came out of the anesthetic and was wheeled through the double doors to the maternity ward.

"Welcome to the Family Birthing Center!" This was the entrance greeting written on the doors.

Even though I was experiencing an overwhelming depth of grief like nothing I had ever felt before, I was recuperating in an area filled with overwhelming joy. As I lay there, tears rolling down my cheeks, my milk started letting down, when I heard the cries of the sweet newborns being wheeled in their bassinets to their new mothers, who anxiously waited to hold their beloved little nurslings to their breasts. Flowers and balloons celebrating the miraculous arrivals abounded. After the many lingering hours of hearing the cries of the babies, coupled with the joy and excitement of all the new parents surrounding me, my husband could see that this whole scene was quite an unbearable burden for me to bear.

He implored, "Can my wife please be released today, instead of tomorrow?"

Without hesitation, my doctor gave the dismissal order, and we were finally on our way home to our other children.

It was Father's Day, which compounded my overindulgence in self-pity.

Bed rest was ordered for a week, since I was still experiencing hemorrhaging. I took up residence on the sofa in the family room during the day, where I could watch my children play. One afternoon I was watching the kids through the big patio window across from me. While Andy squirted water from his mouth, Alyssa pumped his arm as if they were getting water from a well. They were giggling and having so much fun. Yet, I was not even laughing, even though their antics were hilarious.

I was almost indifferent toward my children because I just wanted my baby back. Totally grief-stricken, I felt that all of my insides had been sucked out of me with the procedure used to remove my beloved baby from my womb. I was merely a skeleton with a shell of a body. There was only emptiness inside of me.

My little Alyssa, who was quite a pill, scolded, "You need to get off that couch and quit crying about that baby! You should be worrying about those people in that flood!"

There had been a huge flood in eastern Ohio that June, thus inviting constant coverage of the disaster on television. My four-year-old must have absorbed the news about that tragedy. Of course, Alyssa was right! I should be thinking of others instead of wallowing in my own misfortune and grief.

I resolved to follow my little one's advice after that week of rest. During the day, I tried to be a fun mom again and was back to baking cookies, reading, and playing all day long. I loved my children so much. The joy they brought me was the pinnacle of love, and I knew what I was missing with the loss of my third child. The words Elizabeth Barrett Browning wrote, "I love you to the depth and breadth and height my soul can reach!" was precisely how I felt about motherhood.

At night, though, when my husband and the kids were in bed, I often sat up alone on the couch and cried. My grief consumed me, not allowing me to let go of my sadness at the loss of my baby. For almost a year, my grief did not abate. I longed for my baby. It didn't matter that I didn't even know this precious infant. This child was a one-of-a-kind, unique spirit and soul, just like my other children. I could not even imagine what my life would have been like without my wonderful Andrew and Alyssa. Both of them possess their own incredible personality traits and talents that were predetermined from the moment of conception.

With each passing day, I knew I did not want to continue dwelling in this sorrowful place. Desperately seeking some peace and resolution, I knelt for one of the first times in my thirty-something years of life to pray. Embarrassed to kneel and pray in front of anyone, I went to our bedroom for solace and privacy. With my eyes closed, I knelt at the side of my bed, my hands folded and my head resting in my hands on my bedspread. Earnestly, I prayed to God to please help me understand.

Why did He take my baby, I demanded? He knew how much I loved and treasured my children! I wanted that baby! As I sobbed, I felt my husband's hands on each one of my shoulders, and I felt the love from this compassionate caress give me a feeling of true and absolute peace. I knelt quietly for a few more minutes, savoring that very special moment.

Our bedroom had two doors, one to a half bath that opened to a utility area and on to the kitchen and family room, and the other door to the hallway that led to the other two bedrooms, a full bath, and a formal living room.

I got up and went to the kitchen. Feeling rather embarrassed that Steve had caught me on my knees in prayer, I sheepishly said to him, "Thanks so much for the hug in the bedroom."

"I wasn't in the bedroom, sweetheart?" he replied.

"Yeah! Just now! When you gave me that hug?" I questioned.

"Honey, I wasn't in the bedroom!" Steve exclaimed.

"Well, where is my mom?" I frantically questioned.

"Your mom isn't here, Marlene."

Mom often just came into our home at any given time of day, and so I concluded that she must have walked in and entered our bedroom from the other hallway. Still puzzled, I quickly walked around to the formal living room, looking for my mother. She was not there.

"Well, SOMEONE just hugged me in the bedroom!"

I was freaking out!

"Their hands were right here. Like this on my shoulders." I demonstrated the caress to my husband, placing one hand on each one of his shoulders.

I was absolutely dumbfounded by what had taken place, but amazingly, Steve accepted the whole experience with a matter-of-fact attitude. He simply embraced what had happened at face value. He also thought it was awesome that I had received a physical sign from God that was this special. By contrast, I was overwhelmed with what I had just experienced.

I knew this moment had been real. That touch was such an astonishing sensation, one that I would never forget.

As brokenhearted as I had been since the loss of my child, I knew that I was in my right mind. I wasn't on drugs or drinking alcohol. I rarely even had more than one or two cocktails when we went out. Although I was still grieving, I was working and functioning well, and I wasn't depressed. Unfortunately, I have had to learn how to deal with grief for much of my life. Steve and I thought the touch I felt had to be God, the Holy Spirit, my guardian angel, my dad in Heaven? Or was it Jesus, the divine healer? Something phenomenal had just happened to me, and from that day forward, my grief was completely replaced by profound peace.

I believe that I held that precious baby in such high regard and grieved so deeply over my loss of a child that I had not yet met that God's touching my shoulders was His way of acknowledging my loss. It didn't matter if this child was days, weeks, months, or years old. This child was a unique, eternal soul valued by me and his Creator. In my heart, I realized that God appreciated my knowing what a gift one is given with the life of a precious child.

A mother is just a vehicle, you see. I had a womb for shelter that was temporary. I am me and you are thee, and we have the privilege of carrying a life that is meant to be, here on earth and forever in Heaven. Each life is special, a separate legacy. It is our significant job to tenderly care for that unique life, from womb to tomb, and I take great comfort in knowing that.

I think I, too, might be skeptical if I had heard about an incident like this before my own experience, but it is completely true. There will no doubt, be people who do not believe that this miraculous occurrence happened. Since I was a child, I have always been a "doubting Thomas" myself, and thus, I demanded visible proof for everything from God to Santa Claus to the origin of babies. But, if we believe in God, we will not have even the slightest doubt because we know God has the power to do absolutely anything. After all, millions of Christians worldwide faithfully believe in the virgin birth of Jesus and His rising from the dead.

My hug from Heaven does not mean that I am any more special than any other mother who has experienced the miracle of bringing a life into this world. Nor does it mean that I suffered more than others who lost a child. God just gave me a fearless and outgoing personality that He knew would be willing to share the incredible gift of comfort He offered as a healing blessing to me in my time of need. I am embarrassed that it did take me over twenty years to publicly admit how God consoled me. After this life-changing event, I have always acknowledged that life, from the time of conception, is a gift from God. As long as I live, I will never forget that moment or the feeling of God's touch.

Chapter 4

The Christmas Card
from Heaven

When long-time patient Tania Barnhart's eyes welled with tears, I knew her appointment would not be a typical office visit. I had known her for many years as a patient during my career as a certified paraoptometric. Because she was always very friendly and upbeat, her distressed demeanor made me realize that something was terribly wrong. Almost immediately, she said she had some shattering news to share. Her mother and four other relatives were killed in a horrific van accident in Michigan. Not only did she lose her mother, but she also lost two aunts, and two teenaged cousins. Five family members perished. What an overwhelming tragedy! She told me that her cousin was suffering even more because she had lost both of her children, her mother, and her sister.

How could I even begin to convey my sympathy at a loss of this magnitude? I had developed a special friendship with this wonderful woman over the years and was deeply saddened to hear such a devastating story.

I had known and greatly admired her sweet mother for a number of years as well. Because Tania and her mother were extremely close, she did not know how she was going to be able to go on without her mother. The pain in her eyes left an indelible mark on my heart. Holding her hands, I talked to her for quite some time, trying to reassure her that the love and the bond between a mother and daughter is so strong that her mother would surely be with her now and forever.

Several months later, before the holidays, I was at work, sitting at my desk when I felt this extremely strong urge to send Tania a little note before Christmas. My friend was a very faithful Christian, and I just wanted to let her know that I was thinking of her, especially at this time of year, when I was certain she was desperately missing her mother.

Accordingly, I rose from my desk and walked into the business lounge, where we keep some drawers of cards and stationery that have been stored there for over twenty years! Randomly, I opened a drawer and pulled out a card from among the menagerie of small note cards decorated with a variety of wintry scenes. I then went back to my desk and penned a little handwritten note of sympathy so Tania would know my thoughts were with her this first Christmas without her mother.

As I closed the card to slip it into the envelope, I felt a chill. The name of the train station on this wintry Christmas scene was nothing other than …her mother's name! FLORA! Her mother's name was Flora, a unique name. Not the usual name of a small town from a Norman Rockwell style print. Not Clarksville, or Nelsonville, or some other small town name. There on the sign at the top of the train station was FLORA, certainly not something one would ordinarily see as the name of a train station!

This was most definitely a coincidence too unusual not to be a sign from above. I believe that the bond between a parent and child are eternally linked by God and that often He provides signs to give us comfort and peace while we are here on earth, until we come home to Him and our loved ones in Heaven.

As I have mentioned earlier, there have been numerous instances in my life like the Christmas card episode just described. Each time, God's unique "signs" touched my heart and soul and gave me the strength to go on when I most needed His intervention. These signs came at moments when I was in despair over the precious child that I miscarried or when I was dealing with the illnesses and deaths of loved ones.

One thing I know is that these "kisses from Heaven," as I sometimes call them, occur at a precise moment to convey a positive message of comfort to all of us at a much-needed time. They are truly messages from God. God does not need to send the Angel Gabriel as His messenger to everyone in today's world! In the case of the Christmas card from Heaven, He decided to use me as a vehicle to deliver a mother's love to her grieving daughter.

Chapter 5

A Poem from Heaven

*A*nother one of my life's greatest blessings has been getting to know the tens of thousands of patients I have met over the years. Dr. Frank Tangeman, an optometrist for whom I have worked since he started his practice, recently told me that he has performed 100,000 eye examinations. As a consequence, I have had the pleasure of meeting most of these patients. The majority of them have become personal friends over the years, as we have shared much conversation about their families, jobs, accomplishments, travels, illnesses, joys, and sorrows. One particular patient, Mary Shiverdecker, was a woman I truly enjoyed knowing.

Mary was a very pleasant woman for whom I cared over a number of years. Her daughter, Amy Wade, is, in fact, one of the nicest people I have ever met. I absolutely love her and her genuine and engaging personality. Amy's sweet daughter, Haley, graduated from college, and I now have the pleasure of working with her in our office.

I also knew Mary's son well (Jerry was a personal friend of the doctor I work for), as he would often stop in the office just to sit and talk. A seasoned joke teller, he always had an interesting story to share. This great guy, a master electrician and plumber, was, unfortunately, tragically electrocuted when working on a job at a local country club. Sadly, he left behind a young widow and two beautiful children.

As long as I knew Mary, she and I enjoyed dozens of nice chats together in the office. She possessed this calm and soothing voice that was always comforting to me. I am a very fast-paced, high-energy person who tries to multitask. When my kids were little, I could load the dishwasher, make Kraft macaroni and cheese, bake chocolate chip cookies, talk on the phone, play Monopoly, pray a rosary, do laundry, make a Ghostbuster costume, write a children's book, and nurse a baby, all at the same time. My heart always racing, I am constantly in motion. Mary surely must have known that I needed her calming influence on me. It is somehow very fitting, then, that Mary gave me a copy of the following poem:

My face in the mirror
Isn't wrinkled or drawn!

My house isn't dusty
The cobwebs are gone!

My garden looks lovely
And so does my lawn.

I think I might never
Put my glasses back on!

She included a personal note in her own handwriting, "The poem I spoke about when in the office! Mary Shiverdecker."

I kept this poem in my cluttered desk drawer for years, nestled among the paper clips, post-it notes, rubber bands, candy, and other accumulated articles.

One day when I stumbled upon the note, I smiled as I thought of Mary. Instinctively I had the notion to send it to her daughter, Amy. Quickly, I scribbled a little message to Amy, telling her that I had discovered this poem tucked in my desk and thought she might enjoy having this little verse her mother had shared with me quite some time ago. Thus, I brought it home for my husband to mail and set it on the kitchen counter, where we customarily place outgoing letters.

For several days, Steve asked if he should go the post office to drop the letter to Amy in the mail.

I said, "No, there is no hurry; just mail it tomorrow or next time you are going downtown."

Soon, I received a thank-you card from Amy, complete with a smiley face drawn inside and the handwritten phrase, "You made my day!"

The complete note read:

Marlene,

Thank you so much for the note you found. I received it on the two-year anniversary of the day of her funeral. It was like a sign from Heaven for me & absolutely meant the world to me that you took the time to send it.

Thanks again – Amy

Why I told my husband for several days that he did not need to mail the card to Amy is unclear to me. I usually like to get articles off of the counter. I did not remember what year Mary had died, let alone the month or day. Sometimes God just seems to orchestrate little signs like this to connect grieving loved ones until they meet again. Do not hesitate to perform an act of kindness for others because we never know when God is nudging us to touch someone who needs His reassuring Hand. Perhaps you remember receiving a little message from Heaven at some point in your own life? After all, Heaven comes to us in many subtle ways.

Chapter 6

Not Ready for Heaven

Patrice Victoria (Patty) was the fourth of five daughters born to my mother and father. Her lovely name was very fitting since she was a tall, thin, beautiful blonde with the most gorgeous, ocean-blue eyes and flawless complexion. But, her true beauty emanated from within. She was extremely intelligent, kind, sweet, shy, and impeccably mannered. More significantly, however, she was someone who always put others above herself.

She was a best friend in every sense of the word to her mother and all of her sisters. A fashion diva, Patty loved to shop with her family. I always joked that she knew designers before they knew themselves. No one could find a better bargain than Patty. She literally went through rain, sleet, blizzards, and, yes, even tornados to shop. Driving four or five hours for a day of shopping in Chicago was a small feat. The associates in Saks Fifth Avenue once clapped and cheered for us when we walked into their department store because we were carrying so many purchases. Shopping bags piled to our chins on the drive home deemed a successful trip for the Kessler girls. (Unfortunately, it took quite a large portion of my lifetime to realize the insignificance of material possessions.) Because Patty was so much fun to be around, we laughed until our sides hurt when all of us were together. The excitement and laughter our mother and her four daughters experienced together was immeasurable!

Although we had a blast dancing and partying in our twenties, being lifetime shopping partners, and traveling around the country together, something was truly missing in Patty's life. Her greatest dream was to become a mother, and, at age forty, Patty finally gave birth to an amazing little boy. She was fully immersed in the joyful role of motherhood when life took a complete tailspin.

In September of 2004, I decided to go along with my sister to an appointment to learn the diagnosis from a breast biopsy. The moment Dr. Shanthi Satya entered the examination room, I could tell something was very wrong, even before she summoned those difficult words, "You are such a wonderful person…I am so sorry… you have Stage 3 breast cancer."

You could have picked up my heart from the floor. Patty started crying very hard because she was thinking only of her little boy, the son she waited forty years to love. Despite this extremely devastating pronouncement, she quickly composed herself and never shed a tear again. The day we walked out of that office, the life of my beautiful, blonde, vivacious sister would never again be the same. The life of our entire family would never be the same either.

We immediately converged at our mother's home to deliver the shattering news to our family. Sheila Hawkins, one of Patty's best friends and my mother's neighbor, swiftly stepped in to care for Patty's son while we gained our composure and initiated a game plan. (It would later become such a relief for Patty when Sheila offered child care on numerous occasions throughout Patty's illness.) I began making phone calls at once, starting with my friend, Mindy Dingledine, who was a breast cancer survivor. She highly recommended Dr. R. Thomas Schmidt, a renowned breast surgeon in Indianapolis. Mindy was truly an angel to us on that distressing autumn afternoon. Her kindness and concern led us to the two amazing doctors who would be instrumental in Patty's excellent care.

Without delay, we sought treatment in Indianapolis at The Breast Care Center of Indiana, and, Hematology Oncology of Indiana, about two hours away from our home. Patty was examined by Dr. Schmidt and then placed in a breast cancer research program with Dr. Ruemu Birhiray. With the four trips we made to Indy, we drove almost nine-hundred miles that first week. After her first chemotherapy treatment, my sister had virtually no white count, a 104 degree fever, and sores in her mouth, throat, and on her lips. Her hands were purple and swollen, almost like small boxing gloves, her hair and blackened nails were falling out, and she was getting sick every fifteen minutes, around the clock, for five days. Little did we know that there would be five years of chemotherapy, surgeries, and radiation that would wreak havoc both physically and emotionally. Not only was the physical suffering unbearable, but the emotional anxiety was also devastating. When Patty was diagnosed with breast cancer, her son was just four years old. She would spend the next five years receiving continuous treatment so that she could stay alive for him.

I was inspired by so many other women I met in Dr. Birhiray's office, each enduring their own personal battle with breast cancer. I developed a strong bond of friendship with Rosalie Sullivan, another very courageous mother with a young daughter the same age as Patty's son.

I must take a moment to acknowledge Dr. Ruemu Birhiray, Patty's primary physician in Indianapolis. He is not only an extremely intelligent and incredibly gifted oncologist, but, also, an exceptional man. He truly embraces his patients personally and offers them the compassionate support essential to beat their cancer. Most importantly, he eases their anxiety with his steadfast encouragement. Dr. B. was one of our greatest gifts from God throughout Patty's illness. Dr. Birhiray's wife, Donna, is also a very beautiful and supportive person. His nurses, Dawn Bechara and Leslie Cotton, were instrumental in administering kind, empathetic, and uplifting care to my sister. These dedicated humanitarians lifted the morale of their cancer patients by keeping the chemo room rocking. God's bountiful love was manifested through the tireless devotion of all of these people.

My mother and my two sisters, Marie Eichler and Kathleen Denning, devoted themselves completely to Patty's care. Her health and happiness always came first and foremost in their lives. Mother went to Patty's house to help her every day. Marie and Kathy drove the long distance to Indianapolis countless times in snow, ice, fog, and rain to get their little sister to her treatments. They cared for her and supported her with unparalleled love and devotion. Magnanimously, Kathy went a step further by assuming the surrogate role of full-time mother for Patty's young son, when his mom was in treatment or hospitalized.

The outpouring of support for Patty from our entire community was phenomenal. She received hundreds of cards, frequent meals, gifts, gas cards for travel, and, most importantly, prayers. Her exceedingly considerate friends, neighbors, and Menchhofer in-laws were so thoughtful and generous. The Menchhofer family was so kindhearted that they collected all of the money they could have spent on holiday gifts and presented this enormous sum to Patty at Christmas. (This fine family forgoes gifts for themselves and donates a large sum of money to a person in need every holiday season.) Patty's in-laws remained steadfast to her throughout her illness in countless ways. Mike, Patty's husband, was very fortunate that his employer carried excellent health insurance.

Hair stylist Terri Klosterman, definitely the coolest person on the planet, who would later become a breast cancer survivor herself, styled Patty's hair and wigs throughout her illness at no charge. Terri gave gift certificates for massages, manicures, and pedicures to Patty, my mother, and all of the "Kessler sisters" as well. Equally important, Patty received dozens of cards from two other "Patty" friends. Patty Temple, my sister-in-law, and Patty Schoenleben routinely mailed notes of concern and support throughout my sister's long illness. Her bosses, Mike Gant and Jodie Swaney, offered an open door policy for her to return to work as an insurance agent whenever she desired. It meant so much for her to receive encouragement when her world had suddenly collapsed and she could no longer go to work, go out to eat, or even perform the ordinary everyday tasks that we all take for granted.

Exactly three years after the initial diagnosis, my sister had a recurrence of breast cancer that metastasized to her lungs and bone. Four years after the initial diagnosis, the cancer spread to her liver.

Even as the cancer spread, Patty kept going in a super-human fashion, keeping up a schedule someone in perfect health could not maintain. Amazingly, throughout her terribly aggressive treatment, she was always smiling and graciously thanking her caregivers. She was a tower of strength, never crying or complaining. This incredible strength would shine through in an extraordinary event.

When a scan in December 2008 showed that Patty's cancer in her liver was spreading, she started a new, very aggressive chemotherapy drug. After a month of severe nausea, during which she ate and drank very little, she went to the hospital for an IV to sustain her. After seven hours in the ER, doctors strongly suggested that she be admitted.

For several days, every ten minutes, Patty suffered episodes of what we perceived to be extreme nausea. My husband Steve could time the episodes and know when they were coming on so that we could prepare to help her through them. Later, we learned that these spells were actually air deprivation. In fact, Patty was struggling to breathe. On the third day, at 2:30 in the morning, she sat up gasping for breath and, in clear panic, asked me to call the nurse. The nurse, who came quickly, could not get a pulse. Patty's blood pressure was dropping rapidly.

I looked at Patty's face, and her lips had turned purple. I fearfully exclaimed, "She's not dying, is she?!!!"

At that instant, her eyes rolled back, and the nurse coded her. In just moments, the room was filled with a flurry of doctors and nurses running down the halls from all over the hospital. I was whisked out of the room while the doctors tried to revive her, placing her on a ventilator. Patty had not yet signed the hospital form refusing resuscitation because she so deeply wanted to live for her son. She had the strongest will to live that I have ever witnessed.

I frantically called family and asked the nurse to contact the closest priest. Then, I struggled my way back into the room, dodging the doctors and nurses and climbing over the nightstand, to stand above Patty. I needed to tell her that I was there for her and that I loved her so much.

"It's O.K., Patty. It's O.K." I desperately whispered to her.

The priest, my mother, my sister Marie, and my husband Steve rushed to meet Patty's husband Mike and me within about twenty minutes. The hospital was located about ten miles from our town. Steve had to unlock Mom's home and awaken her in the middle of the night with this shocking news.

We joined the Intensive Care room full of doctors and nurses surrounding the bed working on Patty. Father Tony administered the last rites, after which I requested that we pray the Memorare, which was Patty's favorite prayer. The whole scene was surreal. I watched my baby sister die. Now, I felt as if I were in a dream as we stood in a circle around her body, which was being kept alive with a ventilator.

In the midst of family pouring into the Intensive Care waiting area, several doctors came in to consult with us and to give options for Patty. Patty's husband, Mike, had a very large supportive family, and many of them came as soon as they were notified to join our vigil in the waiting lounge.

All of the medical professionals seemed to be in total agreement that pulling the plug was the humane thing to do. Following hours of consultation with doctors about the best decision for Patty, we decided to remove the ventilator and trust God. I even called our dear friend Dr. Ruemu Birhiray, Patty's oncologist in Indianapolis, who informed us she would likely pass on within two to twenty-four hours. Her suffering would not go on for days. The difficult decision to terminate life support was completed.

When I was alone and awake by Patty's side in the middle of the night, not knowing when she would take her final breath, I was so troubled and afraid. How could our family live without our Patty? My chest and my heart just ached with anxiety. The only noise I often heard came from the oxygen machine, which sounded like flowing water. For some reason, this sound gave me comfort because it made me think of Psalm 23. Alone there with God, I often whispered parts of this soothing Bible psalm, although I did not even know the words completely. I had asked my husband to buy me a Bible over thirty years ago, but I had rarely opened it and seldom read it throughout my life.

Psalm 23:
The Lord is my shepherd;
I shall not want.
In verdant pastures he gives me repose;
Beside restful waters he leads me;
he refreshes my soul.
He guides me in right paths
for his name's sake.
Even though I walk in the dark valley
I fear no evil; for you are at my side
With your rod and your staff
that give me courage.

In the following days, family flew in to share our vigil by Patty's bedside. Sometimes, there were more than a dozen people gathered in the Intensive Care room. Deeply connected by our common sorrow, we shed many tears and made funeral plans. Patty was awake at times, listening to everyone.

My daughter Alyssa immediately flew in from Washington, D.C., and my niece Katie (Eichler) Smith drove up from Columbus. Knowing how little time might remain, they wanted to be with their Aunt Pat, whom they loved so much. They did not leave Patty's side, quenching her dry mouth with syringes of water and applying lip balm to the sores on her lips and baby lotion to the sores on her arms. They even added a little grape juice to the syringes and made "shooters" for her.

Patty murmured, "It has a little kick to it!"

Pampering her with a pedicure and doing her hair and make-up were small gestures of affection offered by Alyssa and Katie for the aunt they adored.

"Get me looking like Heidi!" Patty jokingly requested. "Heidi?" We laughed when she told us she meant super-model Heidi Klum. As I mentioned earlier, Patty was tall, thin, and blonde, with gorgeous blue eyes and a peaches-and-cream complexion, but, she never thought she looked like Heidi Klum.

"It's gonna take a hell of a lot more than this!" she whispered in her weak voice.

Her devoted nieces even conducted a little contest, each of them applying the make-up on only half of Patty's face to see who did the best job. They showed her their professional talents in a mirror both vying for her stamp of approval. Those dear twenty-something girls had reverted to a childhood demeanor to please Patty.

Between immediate family and in-laws, a steady stream of family flowed into Patty's room, wanting to spend their last moments together with her. My brother-in-law, Vern Eichler, a purple heart Vietnam veteran, who himself nearly died after taking six sniper bullets in an ambush and spent many months in the hospital, came to bid a goodbye to Patty. She said she would go on a fishing trip with him, somewhere warm and far, far away. Patty never fished a day in her life! We all exchanged humorous stories with her as we laughed around her bedside.

Other than watching the intense grief expressed by my mom, who was losing her youngest daughter, the most difficult time came when Patty's nine-year-old son came to say goodbye to his mother. He reclined on the hospital bed beside his mother and told her he had to tell her a secret. As he whispered in her ear, Hollywood movie writers could not have scripted a more emotional moment. This moment reminded me of the movie "Love Story," in which Ryan O'Neill lies down on the hospital bed beside the love of his life, Ali McGraw, to say his goodbye. Patty told her son that angels are like people and are always with us.

One night Patty said, "I don't know where Heaven is?" Coming from a family of champion shoppers, I joked that Heaven is eternal shopping at the Mall of the Universe, where everything is 75% off or free and there is Graeter's ice cream and Cheesecake Factory everyday.

Patty said, "Hmmm…my family (she held one palm out)… Cheesecake Factory and Graeter's…" as she held both palms out evenly.

Then she said, "Set an extra place, a fifth place, when you go to Cheesecake Factory or Graeter's. And order me a sundae with two scoops!" Was she saying she wasn't going to be here? Nevertheless, two days later, Patty was sitting up in bed, saying she had to go home and get to her chemotherapy appointment in Indianapolis in a few days!

When I was in the hospital cafeteria the next day, a nurse, Evie Eaton, came up to me and said, "Do you know you experienced a miracle? I have been a nurse my whole life, and people just do not survive the cardiac tamponade that your sister did! Praise the Lord!"

I realized at that moment that no one is in control of the time of his passing. God has a plan for everyone's birth and death. He gives life and ends life at a destined moment that suits His timing.

Several days later, my husband went to pick up our dear friend, Father Angelo Caserta, who lived about an hour away. This small-framed priest of Sicilian immigrant parents, donning a black wool topcoat and large brimmed hat, made quite an entrance walking into the hospital. In spite of his diminutive size, Father Angelo always exudes an enormous presence.

As Father walked down the halls to Patty's room, he appeared to be a man with an urgent mission at hand. Once he entered the room, he joined hands with us around Patty's bed and began to pray. It was Father Ang at Patty's side, then my mother, my husband at the foot of the bed, and my sister Kathy and me at the other side. After we prayed together, Father fell into a deep, sacred silence. He then anointed Patty's forehead and body with a consecrated host. It was probably one of the most amazing spiritual experiences of my life. This extraordinary man is such a saintly person. I could write a book about his life of devotion to God and the multitude of miraculous and inexplicable events attributed to him. Father Ang is deeply beloved by a massive number of adoring friends and followers from all over the country. I have never met anyone who could compare to his loving and generous nature.

After Father Caserta left, I went home briefly. I was reluctant to end my nine-day vigil for fear that something bad might happen in my absence. To my astonishment, when I came back, Patty was walking around the floor with the help of a walker, and her oxygen, catheter, and all of her IV's had been removed. The swelling from the thirty pounds of fluid she had amassed was receding. Her body was suddenly functioning normally, and she was eating! What I was witnessing was hope fulfilled and rewarded. More than that, Patty's return to life was an incredible miracle.

My sister Marie, who is a world champion shopper much like Patty and my mom, was always bringing presents up from the hospital gift shop. Marie bought out every hospital gift store where Patty had been a patient! After Patty's unexpected recovery, Marie's gifts were even more in evidence. My daughter Alyssa also got into the spirit of giving. Because it was now March, Alyssa bought a shamrock plant in the gift shop for Patty. Despite being left outside in the snow and freezing cold on the porch, that shamrock thrived for many years.

Not to be outdone, Marie found these cute little animal puppets in the gift shop. With good-humored enthusiasm, she put on a puppet show for Patty. Marie would stand behind the hospital curtain and the puppet, Bunkey, would talk to Patty. Marie was absolutely hilarious.

During Patty's time in the hospital, I slept in a recliner beside her. In the early morning hours one day, Patty had another frightening episode. Terrified myself, I called Steve, Marie, and Alyssa. They immediately rushed to the hospital. All of us were up with Patty throughout the night. We ended up putting on a 3:45 A.M. puppet show for her, laughing until we cried! Alyssa said, "This is the red eye show!" Steve was the light man. We joked about putting shows on at 1, 3, and 5 P.M. for the hospital and selling tickets and concessions. What a crazy family we must have seemed!

After Patty survived this critical period, she went on to spend four more months with her son and family. She savored warm summer days at the swimming pool, laughing and sunbathing with girlfriends Barb Harter and Karrie Hoyng, while they all enjoyed watching their children splashing in the water. There were shopping excursions with her mom and sisters, including her 50th birthday brunch in Columbus. On that special occasion, Patty received a Tiffany necklace from her loving family. Steve and I even drove Patty and our nephew to Chicago because she desperately wanted to bring her young son on one more trip. During this outing, we feasted on warm beignets at Grand Lux Café, munched on Garrett's Caramel Corn (our favorite Windy City treat), shopped on Michigan Avenue, and thrilled at the sight of spectacular fireworks at Navy Pier. Despite her terminal illness, Patty remained happy and upbeat throughout this mini trip. Even though Patty was mostly confined to a wheel chair by then, she insisted on walking as much as possible. Nothing could defeat her indomitable spirit. Still, I sensed a deep sadness within her when she hesitated to leave our last stop at The Field Museum to depart for home. She knew in her heart that she would never be back.

One week later, which was four months after Patty died and came back to life in March, her condition necessitated surgery to drain fluid from around her heart. The day after coming home from heart surgery in Indianapolis, she slipped into an unconscious state and passed on to Heaven six days later. Many signs from God and angels occurred the week that she died.

I learned many things from my sister and her courageous, five-year battle with breast cancer. The most important thing I learned is that God is always in control of our lives on earth. He is the only one who gives life and ends our time in this world. I also learned that the human spirit often prevails against unimaginable suffering or seemingly impossible obstacles. To my own surprise, I discovered that I could forge onward with a smile and find joy in each day, despite the fact that everything in my life seemed to be falling apart. Finally, I learned that God is truly present with a deeper love and compassion than I ever imagined to be possible.

My favorite quote from Mother Teresa is, "See the face of God in everyone you meet." I believe that you will then treat everyone as if they were God himself. For five years, my amazing family dedicated every day to caring for Patty and her young son. During that period, we saw God's face in her suffering face every day, and my whole family learned a love and empathy for others that changed our lives.

We should thank God every day for our own health and blessings and, in turn, help others who are sick, poor, or in need. Unfortunately, we sometimes seek large bank accounts and material things, failing to realize until it is too late that those are the least important things in life. There is no greater gift from God than the people we love and the time we are given to express that love. "Use the beautiful gifts God has given you for His greater glory. All that you have and all that you are and all that you can be and do...." Mother Teresa

This following is one of my "silly poems" that I wrote to my sister on her 49th birthday, the year before she died. I just had to write a poem to show Patty how much she meant to me. Write a "poem" or your feelings about how much a person means to you. One need not be a talented writer to speak from the heart. God will always give us the words. My dad often wrote notes to me on his business cards, which he would then place next to my school lunch money. Some of these I cherish dearly over thirty years after he died. His love still shines through his personal scribbled handwriting, "Beane, I am happy when you are happy...Love, Dad"

HAPPY BIRTHDAY PATTY!

We are one and the same, sisters are we
From the same mother's womb we came to be.

You are part of my own heart and soul
And without you, I would not be whole.

From our shared childhood, when you were nicknamed
little Pooh
To your own motherhood, when we watched your
baby coo.

We share many fun memories of vacations together
Sitting by the pool and walking the beach in sunny
weather.

We will have many more years to share laughter and to
    shop
We will be saggy old ladies before one of us drop!

For every joy you have had, I have felt it just as bold
For every tear you've shed, I have cried it one hundred
    fold.
There is nothing or no one any dearer to me
Because you are the best sister there could ever be.

Patty, I love you more than any words could ever say
So, I pray to God and thank Him for you every day!

Love,
Beane (my nickname)

Chapter 7

Christ Came From Heaven

*B*ecause I have had many experiences of Heaven coming to me in my life, I believe God wants me to share them. As a lifelong Christian, but certainly one who would never outwardly express my common and ordinary faith, I am now compelled to share the most profound visual experience in my life.

Everyone must bear crosses in their lives. So, like all others, I have borne my own. But, God has a purpose for everything that happens in our lives. I was extremely blessed to be given a very tangible sign as a personal acknowledgement from God that He knew and understood my family's pain.

These personal messages are meant to give us reassurance that there is a God and that love and goodness always comes from Him in the end. While the horrible five-year struggle and heartache my family endured will forever be a part of me, it will also be an enduring sign of love from God.

I have finally realized that this life is not meant to be Heaven because it is full of pain and suffering, be it physical or emotional. God did not make Himself immune from what we humans experience during our lifetime on earth. He Himself experienced watching His only Son suffer the most unbearable passion and agonizing death imaginable. This historical moment has been retold throughout the world for thousands of years. This ultimate sacrifice would change lives for all eternity.

During my sister Patty's five-year battle with breast cancer, I watched human suffering at its worst. As I have mentioned previously, after her first chemotherapy treatment, she had virtually no white count, a 104 degree fever, and sores in her mouth, throat, and on her puffy lips. The poor girl's hands were purple and swollen, almost like small boxing gloves; her hair and blackened nails were falling out, and she was getting sick every fifteen minutes around the clock for days. She could not eat anything, and nothing came out of her except some black, unrecognizable gel substance.

Little did we know that there would be five more years of chemotherapy, surgeries, and radiation that would be physically and emotionally grueling. Incredibly, my sister always lived with an unbounded grace, strength, and faith throughout her ordeal, without ever complaining. As if to defy her adversary, she always dressed like a designer fashion diva, even when she had chemotherapy appointments. Her defiance of her cancer was punctuated with her decision to shop after her treatments, no matter how bad she felt. I once remember propping her on a display in the Ralph Lauren store because she was so weak she could hardly walk.

From the moment this advanced stage of cancer was diagnosed, it soon became apparent that the only power we could turn to was God. We pulled out all the stops! Patty, my mother, and my family and I went to Mass, spent time in prayer with our beloved friend Father Angelo Caserta (we were led to this devout priest by the extraordinarily gifted Radio Maria personality Francesca Franchina), prayed the rosary daily, and committed to many novenas. My daughter in Washington, D.C., even prayed a novena with us via cell phone while she was traveling on the Metro. Without hesitation, we willingly exchanged our Tiffany necklaces to wear blessed medals of Padre Pio and St. Peregrine –"good ole Pergy" I called him. My husband shook his head and chuckled as I prayed along with the rosary on EWTN nightly, occasionally switching back and forth to "Sex and the City" to see who Carrie Bradshaw was dating when Mother Angelica had a long pause reciting the Hail Mary!

My mother and I went to Mass and communion nearly every day for five years to pray for my sister. I must confess that this devotion was not always done with a smile on my face. Readily, I admit that I am no Mother Teresa, although she is one of my most admired persons.

During Patty's illness, I never got enough sleep and was, as a result, forever tired. Predictably, I often grumbled because

I had to get up an extra hour earlier than usual to get to Mass before work. I seriously acted as if I were doing God a favor, forgetting what He had done for me!

Quite a few times, when I left home at 7:20 A.M. on a cold and dark, wintry morning, I would complain and even swear that I had put up with just about enough of this #*#* #*#*! (On my best day, if I spilled a gallon of milk on the floor, fiddlesticks probably would not be the word of choice!) Yes, shamefully, I cussed out God on more than one occasion because I was so ticked off at Him about our hopeless situation.

As I headed out each day, it was too early to hear the Beatles, Katie Perry, or my favorite Coldplay song "Viva la Vida." So, I would settle for number nine on my CD player, Louis Armstrong's "What a Wonderful World." As I looked around at the dark and silent morning, listening to this incredible one-of-a-kind voice, I felt a measure of peace. I despised Ohio winters, but the beauty and stillness of a gentle snowfall illuminated by the dim light of the street lamps at dawn was truly serene.

Many days, as I went to my pew in the back of church after communion, I looked intently at the Pieta, the huge statue of the Blessed Mother holding her Son's crucified body.

"You only had to watch your Son suffer for three hours, and my mother has had to watch her daughter suffer for five years!" I whispered to myself.

I actually had the gall to criticize God many times. But, somehow deep down, I still always knew God felt and understood my family's pain. Not to my surprise, we did indeed experience the miraculous Hand of God repeatedly throughout my sister's illness.

During the week that my sister died, my mother and I stayed with her around the clock. At night, I also slept in the same bed, by her side. I did not want her to be alone or afraid if she ever woke up. Most importantly, I did not want her to die alone. I wanted her to feel my love at the last moment of her existence on this earth. She was in a comatose state by then, lying motionless with labored breathing, never awakening or uttering a word the entire week. Then, one night when my mother and I were alone with her, she started an agonizing ordeal that began exactly at twelve o'clock and ended precisely at the hour of three o'clock. My mother and I were frantic as we tried unsuccessfully to ease her pain and suffering.

In desperation, we called the hospice nurses, and, with their professional advice, exhausted all of our resources of assistance to no avail. I administered a syringe of the most powerful drug at our disposal, but it did not give any relief. We were both literally kneeling on the bed at her feet, emotionally spent, as we watched her body thrashing about and writhing with pain. Later, I reflected how utterly helpless we were. How did Christ's mother, Mary, and Mary Magdalene survive when they knelt in total despair at the foot of the cross?

Finally, Patty cried out in what sounded like a man's voice in a foreign language! She opened her eyes for the only instant that entire week and looked heavenward. Then, suddenly, at precisely three o'clock, both of her arms flung straight out horizontally to the side. At the same time, her feet were crossed, while her head dropped to her shoulder and the tube from her side was gushing with water.

My mother could not believe her eyes as she exclaimed, "Oh, my God! She looks like Christ on the cross!"

At that moment, an overwhelming feeling unlike anything I had ever experienced before in my life came over me. Surely, there will never again be a more compelling moment in my life. I now knew that God was telling me He was responsive to my sister's suffering and, therefore, our torment as well. He had seen every single second of Patty's excruciating pain and our corresponding despair throughout the five long years of Patty's travail. He had heard my snide remarks directed to His mother, the Blessed Virgin Mary, when I glared at the statue of the Pieta in the back of church and my foul-mouthed and bitter complaints fired straight at Him for our distressing situation. But, more importantly, I knew He had heard our heartfelt prayers that continued daily and faithfully, despite our anger and frustration.

In retrospect, I cannot even imagine what an ultimate sacrifice God endured when His own Son suffered and died for us. What torture and sorrow the mother of God must have endured watching the passion and death of her only beloved Son. As I witnessed, firsthand, the heartbreak my own mother felt as she watched her daughter's final struggle, I knew Patty's suffering, as torturous as it was, could not begin to compare with Christ's suffering on the cross. And yet, in a small but miraculous way, I felt God allowed my devoted mother to share Mary's maternal sufferings at the Crucifixion.

The most amazing aspect of Patty's final ordeal and its uncanny resemblance to the Crucifixion was the timing. What would be the likelihood of Patty's greatest agony beginning at the exact time that Christ's final three hours of suffering on the cross started and ending at precisely the same time that Christ died? It could have happened from one until four, two until five, three until six, or numerous combinations of hours and minutes totaling three hours, but, it did not. It occurred between the hours of twelve and three. Routinely, I documented her symptoms and charted the time I dispensed her medications. There is no doubt that I looked at the hands of the clock on the nightstand at the exact moments her ordeal started and ended. These times will be permanently etched in my mind. At three o'clock that morning, when her agony abruptly ended, she immediately went back to lying motionless, the way she had been all week. Patty remained totally still right up until the moment she peacefully died over a day later.

When I consider Patty's unimaginable three hours of suffering, as well as my other unique personal experiences, I am convinced of the truth of the wise and discerning words spoken by Father Caserta, "There is no chance, no coincidence, or luck." In other words, God's sovereignty is involved in all matters of this world. All things take place under His will, and nothing is a matter of mere chance.

Insurmountable goodness and love came from Christ's sacrifice on the cross. Goodness and love would come from my sister's suffering as well. When we take up our own crosses in this life and still keep faith and trust in God, we are true witnesses to Him. We can be assured He knows of our devotion and that He will reward us.

The lesson in all of this is that God wants us to see His face in everyone we meet. I saw the face of Christ in my sister's suffering and death. God wants us to see His face not only in the sick and dying but also in all of those who suffer. We must seek God's face in the homeless person, the orphaned child, the wounded veteran, the drug addict, the aged and lonely, the bullied classmate, the prisoner, the immigrant, and the hungry and poor throughout the world.

God revealed to me and my mother on that fateful night that He sees the heartaches and sufferings of all His children. He cannot wait for us to join Him in paradise for eternal bliss and joy, free from further suffering.

When I was a child, having grown up in a predominantly Christian area, the world seemed to stop from twelve until three on Good Friday. It was eerie to me because stores and businesses closed, and the town seemed to be so still that it appeared like darkness and gloom must have presided over the whole earth for those three hours.

It was mandatory for students in our parochial school to go to all services at Immaculate Conception during those devoted hours. It was torture for most kids to kneel in church for that long because we did not understand the magnitude of what Christ had done for us through His suffering on the cross. I remember going to Linda Rose's slumber party on Holy Thursday in fifth grade and then having to go to church on Good Friday for three hours. Being up all night with no sleep, I actually thought I was the one who was suffering!

Sadly, it seems now as though even many Christians regard this day as any other ordinary day. Stores are certainly not closed. In fact, Good Friday is actually one of the busiest days to buy groceries, candy, and new spring clothes. I plead "mea culpa" as I have often gone to the mall shopping if I had Good Friday off work. I should be ashamed that I put my love of T.J. (Maxx) above J.C. (Jesus Christ)!

When I was a little girl, Easter Sunday meant a pretty new dress, hat, white gloves, and patent leather shoes for Mass. It also meant hunting for pastel-colored eggs and enjoying a basket full of jelly beans, marshmallow Peeps, a chocolate rabbit and Esther Price chocolates (a delectable family favorite), followed by a big family dinner with all the china and crystal in the formal dining room. When I would hear the Volkswagen van pulling in the driveway with the Dayton kids (our thirteen cousins), I would run upstairs to hide my Easter basket before my candy instantly vanished before my eyes. Normally, I was not stingy!

Easter will always hold a totally new and profound meaning for me. God gifted me with a miracle that connected my life to His divinity for a mere moment. After my own intense glimpse of Jesus on the cross, He will always be my first thought as the true meaning of Easter. As I contemplate Christ on the cross, I see only the greatest love there ever was or ever will be.

Chapter 8

The Cell Phone Call
From Heaven

My sisters and I are like a web, with tight-knit love and numerous indelible memories woven among all of us. Because we have always been very close, we are bound together by a bond not easily broken. In particular, Patty, being the baby of the family, had an extremely close tie to all of her big sisters.

Indeed, there could not be a closer connection between two people than the one Patty and I shared. We shared a womb, our childhood memories, our clothes, our hopes, dreams, and fears. She was constantly there for me, through the highs and lows, from my joyous wedding and the birth of my children to the devastating death of our father and the miscarriage of my last child. Patty was my soul sister, not just my biological sister.

I once heard on a T.V. show that a Hollywood star and her mother had made a pact that whoever of them died first, she would give the other a sign from Heaven that only the two of them would recognize. This idea sounded crazy to me! Hmmm…could that ever work? I was certainly very skeptical about the prospect of such communication from beyond, but I shared the concept with Patty and joked that we needed to try it someday.

I often chuckled that I would send her a bunch of bananas when I died since it was a family joke that I ate bananas every day. Invariably, I brought along a banana or two for a snack when we went on a trip, a girl's weekend, or even an out-of-town shopping day with my sisters. The traveling banana usually came home brown and uneaten because it ranked in last place to Graeter's ice cream or one of my other favorite treats. Actually, one time we were parked at Graeter's in Columbus, and the banana I had packed got too ripe in the car. Unluckily, one of my sisters sat on it and discovered mashed banana all over the seat of her pants when she got out of the car. We laughed hysterically, but this innocent mishap prompted me to stop bringing a banana along for a snack!

Recalling "the sign from Heaven" pact between the Hollywood celebrity and her mother, I decided that sending a bunch of bananas was not very unique. After all, anyone could send a fruit basket, including bananas, as a token of sympathy, and, as a result, there was no way for my sister to know that I was trying to communicate with her. No, whatever sign we agreed upon would be our own little secret, something no one else would ever know or be able to duplicate. This whole idea was only a silly, fleeting thought many years ago because I never dreamed one of us would not live a long life, especially since longevity runs in our family. Now, in retrospect, maybe our silliness was more of a premonition than I could ever have envisioned.

As I have already detailed, my sister fought a horrendous five-year battle with breast cancer. The years of chemotherapy, surgeries, and radiation both physically and emotionally exhausted her. Despite her agony, Patty always lived with an incredible grace, strength, and faith throughout her ordeal, never once complaining.

During Patty's numerous hospital stays, there were many consecutive days and nights that I did not sleep at all while I was tending to her needs. Although I was miserably tired, I reminded myself that I was the one who was so blessed to be spared her unimaginable pain and insurmountable discomfort. Still because I loved her so much, I felt as though I would physically identify with her pain much of the time.

I would often think of Christ and how no one would stay up with Him throughout His agony in the garden, and I would then quietly whisper, "I will stay up for you Christ, through Patty." Don't ever miss the opportunity to help someone who is suffering. Your sacrifice for one of God's children will not go unnoticed.

Only about a month before her five-year-survivor milestone, Patty fell into a comatose state, lying motionless with labored breathing, before we could ever discuss our little idea and make a final game plan. She was always so determined to survive that we never talked about the alternative.

Over the past five years, I had always stayed with her, around the clock, throughout her numerous emergency room visits, surgeries, and hospital stays. There was no way I was leaving her now. After four days, my brother-in-law Dick insisted he would stay beside her while I went home and showered. Dick had stayed with me during Patty's many long nights in the emergency room throughout her illness and I could always count on him. I hesitated to leave, but there did not seem to be any change. With some reluctance, I agreed to go home for a brief respite.

I went home and put my phone in the hard leather case (something I never did) and set it on the kitchen counter. When I came out of the shower, I heard my phone ringing. Quickly wrapping a towel around me, I ran from the bedroom to answer it. It was my sister-in-law, Patty Temple.

"Marlene, did you call me?" she questioned.

"No?" I responded.

I am close to my sister-in-law, but it is rare for us to call each other on our cell phones. As we spoke, I heard a beep announcing an incoming call.

Abruptly, I uttered, "I have to go! It could be Dick calling me about Patty!"

The call was from Dick, who said that I should come right over to my mother's home, where we had been caring for Patty. We had moved Mom to a smaller home, just a few blocks from me, several years ago. Frantically, I flew out the door and made a beeline to my mother's house in about a minute flat.

When I walked in the front door, I immediately sensed something was wrong and was informed that my beloved sister had passed while I was gone. I was so devastated that I had been with her constantly for so many days and weeks in the hospital over the years, and, yet, I was not with her when she took her last breath. Understandably, I was very distressed that I had left her side when she probably needed me most.

In the hour that I waited for the funeral director to arrive to take her body, I contemplated that four other women in the United States had died of breast cancer in that time period. Four other mothers collapsed with grief at the loss of their daughters; four other children suffered devastation at the loss of their mothers; four other husbands felt the loss of their life partners', and four other sisters experienced the intense pain I felt at the loss of their sisters.

I now knew the depth of grief only a sister could feel when she lost the person who shared the same womb, the same house, the same clothes, the same memories, the same hopes and dreams, and the same laughter and the deepest sorrows.

When the funeral director asked me, "Do you want to leave when we take her body?"

I simply replied, "No."

"Do you want to have her body covered when we take her out?"

I simply replied, "Yes."

Then I watched as they carried her body on the stretcher to the white hearse waiting in the street. She would never come back to my mother's home again. More profoundly, she would never share her life with me again.

Patty passed away at 8:14 A.M., as documented by the hospice nurse. A short time later, I opened my cell phone to start making calls to relatives, and I see...Call from Patty... at EXACTLY 8:14 A.M.! Not 8:13 or 8:15, but exactly her precise time of death, 8:14! This phone call was my sign from her! It was like a phone call from Heaven, sent directly to me.

This occurrence was too unusual not to be my special sign. After all, my phone was in the hard leather case on the counter while I was in the shower, so I did not call my sister-in-law, Patty Temple. My numbers are listed in alphabetical order... Alyssa, Andy... and Patty Temple is way down the list. If I had accidentally "pocket dialed" a phone number, I probably would have hit one of the first numbers, but, in fact, I did not call Patty Temple or anyone else.

I also did not touch or use my phone while I was at home showering. How my sister-in-law saw a call from me or thought I called and, in turn, called me so that I saw... "Call from Patty"... come up on my phone at the exact time of Patty's death, was surely divine intervention. What else could God have done to offer me a sign that Patty was in Heaven other than "A Call from Patty," especially since we had not had time to devise our secret plan?

Knowing that I was so devastated by my sister's terrible suffering and death, I truly believe God blessed me with this tangible little sign that she was now with Him in Heaven. Her suffering was truly over. God blessed our family with a sign for our family's devotion to Him despite our loss.

I have been very blessed to have Heaven come to me on many occasions throughout my life. Look for the ways Heaven has come to you in your life. God comforts us in both large and small ways. Usually, He does so through the love of others, nature, animals, and all of His creation. In this case, God even used a cell phone!

Chapter 9

A Quiet Passage to Heaven

My mom, at age eighty-seven years young, acted more like a fifty-year-old. Her mind and memory were sharp, and she could still "shop 'til you drop." She had a bridge club and played cards twice a week. When she started to become fatigued and had no energy, I assumed she just must be starting to age. Her family, however, had longevity on both her mom and dad's sides, so I thought she would live to be one-hundred years old, like so many of her relatives. After all, her cousins ride roller coasters and motorcycles when they are over one-hundred years old! Moreover, Mom had barely been sick a day in her life. We did take her to the doctor for at least four appointments, but nothing was diagnosed, despite running blood work.

I saw my mom almost every day of my life. We moved her from a large nine-room home where our family grew up to a smaller two-bedroom home several blocks away from me. Usually, Mother came to our home for dinner after I came home from work. Since my office was open late hours, I am extremely lucky that my husband has a wonderful meal ready every night when I arrive home. After dinner, we all routinely watched NBC news together, and she watched "Wheel of Fortune" and "Jeopardy." Often, we talked and caught up on our days while I did some household chores. Mom's grandson would then go home with her to spend time with her and play cards.

On one particular Thursday, Mother did not want to come over for dinner, so I stopped at her house. She was so weak that I told her I was afraid she might fall. I insisted she spend the night at our home, even though she resisted. My husband and I had previously talked and agreed that Mom could live with us, if necessary, someday because Steve works out of our house with his own optical laboratory, Sommer Optical. Thus, he would always be home for her while I was at work every day.

The second night she stayed with us, I was very concerned and stayed up with her through the night. At one point when I was helping her to the bathroom, she became so weak I was scared she might die.

As I sat beside her on the bed in the middle of the night, she said, "I think I have leukemia and I am going to die."

"That is absurd, Mother! You do not have leukemia, and you are not going to die!" I shot back.

Where had she gotten such a crazy idea? No one in our family history has ever had cancer, that is, until my sister developed breast cancer. Mother had been to the doctor several times, but the possibility of cancer had never been considered. To me, Mom's sudden self-diagnosis was ridiculous.

I called Mom's cardiologist the next morning. An old neighbor and a personal friend, he told me to take her to the emergency room at St. Rita's in Lima, a hospital about forty-five minutes away, because they would have a hematologist and a nephrologist on staff. Recently, an ultrasound at a local hospital had detected a cyst on Mom's kidney. This cyst was assumed to be benign. Also, a few gallstones were discovered, but nothing earth-shattering was found.

Two of my sisters and I took off for Lima with Mom as soon as possible that Saturday morning. When we arrived at the emergency room, the hospital staff took care of us right away even though forty-nine ER rooms were filled with patients. Taking it all in stride, Mom was her usual kind, positive, upbeat and sweet personality.

The nurses and doctors were wonderful. They immediately started doing blood profiles and all kinds of tests for hours. During the process, they noted the terrible rash, resembling blood blisters, all over her chest, trunk, and back.

Finally, two doctors, wearing very concerned looks on their faces, delivered Mom's test results. They gravely stated, "We can transport your mother to The James in Columbus or to The Cleveland Clinic."

With stunned looks on our faces, we wondered what the heck was going on. It had to be cancer! I was shocked! The

James is the renowned cancer treatment center in Columbus, Ohio, only a few hours away. The world-famous Cleveland Clinic is four hours away from our home.

Mom's white count was 134,000, instead of a normal range of eight to ten thousand. She was diagnosed with acute myeloid leukemia. The doctors wanted to know why a CBC (complete blood profile) had not been taken recently and faxed from our local hospital. A CBC that had been administered in September was normal. Clearly, this disease had come on very quickly.

Because we needed time to absorb this terrible news and to help our mother make decisions on a treatment plan, we declined transport to another hospital. Immediately, doctors began blood transfusions and admitted Mom. This news was a tremendous blow, not only to our dear mom but to her whole family. We spent the week at the hospital with Mom as she received blood transfusions, all the while helping her to cope with this news. Throughout, she remained the rock she has always been, never shedding a tear. Ironically, Mom was far more in control of her emotions than her family was.

I relied on the support and spiritual guidance of Father Caserta once again. He consoled me and prayed for Mother for over an hour via my cell phone at St. Rita's Hospital.

One evening when I stayed overnight, I was talking to her in the middle of the night.

"Why did you tell me you thought you had leukemia that night at my house?"

She said she knew someone diagnosed with leukemia who suffered a rash similar to hers.

"Why didn't you tell me? I never knew that was a symptom of leukemia?"

I felt so bad because I worked in the health care field, and, therefore, I thought I knew quite a bit about diseases and health-related issues. However, I suspected nothing. "Petechiae" is the term for the dark red pin-point blood blisters that covered my mother's chest and back.

Mom was dismissed six days later on a Friday, and we moved her to my home to care for her. I called Dr. Ruemu Birhiray, my sister's amazing oncologist in Indianapolis, who had become our close family friend. I left a message, to which he responded as soon as he could.

With true compassion in his voice, he said, "Oh, Marlene, I am so sorry."

He explained that a bone marrow transplant or chemotherapy treatment at her age would not be recommended. Even undergoing blood transfusions would be grueling for her and take time away from her family. Given her diagnosis, he gave me the shattering news that she could die within a span of two days to two weeks. I was crushed by this pronouncement.

My sisters and I decided to set up my house for Mom's care. We were equipped with oxygen, a commode, wheelchair, and a wedge for her bed. Within a few days, simply moving her with a wheelchair became quite a chore. We realized that we needed visiting nurses, and so, adding a hospital bed, we transformed our great room into the center of her care. Nurse Maria Suhr was an absolute blessing as she guided us toward the end of our mother's life.

Instantly, our home became a bee hive of activity. In addition to my husband and me, there was our son and our daughter, who had flown in from Washington, D.C. to be with us. My fourteen-year-old nephew, the son of my sister, Patty, who had died from breast cancer, was at our home daily as well. My two sisters and their husbands, and another granddaughter from Columbus added to the list of regular visitors. Mom's brother, Mark Klosterman, longtime Probate Judge for our county, came faithfully each day to comfort his sister. Both he and an older brother to Mom were brokenhearted.

Mom's nephews drove two hours from Columbus one evening, making the trip as soon as they heard about their beloved aunt. One of the nephews had suffered a stroke just recently but was still determined to make the drive to visit his aunt. They loved their Aunt Sally deeply. Her sister-in-law Diane, Mark's wife, was also very close to Mom. Mom's ninety-year-old brother Cy and his wife Ann from Dayton, both battling cancer themselves, made the trip with three more nephews and nieces. It was touching to see Mom's ninety-year-old brother giving her a foot massage. Mother dearly loved her brothers and sisters-in-law.

More nieces and nephews from several hours away came to visit the next day. Our house became a hub of adoring relatives and friends wanting to be with their sister, aunt, and friend.

My sisters and I were serving pie and coffee to the relatives. All of us were eating pizza and drinking beer, wine, and champagne. Meanwhile, homemade casseroles and desserts were being delivered from neighbors, friends, and relatives. In the midst of all of the activity, visiting nurses were coming and going regularly.

Florists delivered many beautiful flower arrangements to our home for Mother. Phone calls from friends and relatives throughout the country came around the clock. I often put the phone to Mother's ear so that she could hear the love and well wishes from the voices of those who treasured her. Fr. Kenneth Schnipke, our Immaculate Conception parish priest, came to offer the Anointing of the Sick with his calm and soothing voice. Circling closely around our mother, our family was privileged to participate in the administration of this beautiful sacrament. Even our Goldendoodle, Mo, nudged his way into the group to join this last sacred ritual for Grandma.

My most touching memory during Mother's illness came when my children insisted that I lie down to rest one night while they tended to their grandmother. While caring for Mom, I had not slept more than several hours a night for the past week. It was about two o'clock in the morning when I was forced to go lie down on our bed in the room across the hall from my mom. Unable to sleep, I just listened as the kids lovingly and tenderly nursed for their grandmother.

Both of my kids have achieved many personal and academic goals in their lives, but nothing could make me prouder than knowing the considerate and empathetic adults they have become. On this night, I laughed and I cried and I beamed with pride at their humanity and compassion. When I returned to the room, I saw Alyssa sitting at the head of the bed, with her legs spread and Grandma propped between them while she rubbed Mom's painful back.

Later, I smiled and shook my head as I heard Alyssa loudly crushing ice with a wooden rolling pin at 4 A.M. to feed Grandma ice chips. It touched my heart to hear Andy carefully and gently lifting his grandmother with her arms around his neck, making sure he wasn't hurting her in the process. They were both on top of the situation, reminding me when to administer morphine with a syringe or to give other drugs to relieve pain. Leaving nothing undone, they fed Mom popsicles and adjusted the fan to keep her cool from the hot flashes of AML. Though Mother had no appetite, one night she did take one spoonful of her favorite treat, Graeter's black raspberry chip ice cream.

Sensing that the end was near, we pretty much kept a constant vigil at our mother's side. The afternoon she died, all three of her daughters and their husbands, along with four of her grandchildren, were present in our great room with her.

My mother, like her own mother, prayed the rosary daily, although her deep faith was certainly tested throughout the suffering and death of her daughter. Before Mom passed, my sister Kathy sat beside her praying the rosary. The moment Kathy put Mom's rosary in her right hand and her youngest grandson took her left hand into his, Mother took her last breath. It was the perfect passing for our mother. She was a humble person, and this passage, free of fanfare, was befitting for her entrance into Heaven. Mom died on November 20, 2013, just five days after moving her to my home.

Most people do live ordinary lives without fanfare and without the power of coincidental and tangible signs from Heaven that God sometimes sends to reveal Himself. Because my mother was such a special person, I often thought that when she died I would witness the biggest revelation of all from God. I have experienced about a half-dozen extremely profound signs from God associated with the death of loved ones. Mom's departure from this earth would surely be awe-inspiring to me, complete with some personal affirmation from God that, "Yes, there is a God!" and "Yes, there is a Heaven!"

Since I have been blessed with such extraordinary signs from God on numerous occasions, I guess I had the notion that I would receive an earth-shattering cue that my amazing mother was definitely with God. Did I think the Heavens would part and that trumpets would blare? Would white doves fly out of the pearly gates in huge flocks? A chariot driven by white horses would surely provide her a personal escort to meet God through a crimson-colored sky filled with double rainbows? Would it take something this spectacular to announce the arrival of my beloved mother to Heaven?

Of course, I am joking about this phenomenal opening of the gates of Heaven, but I must have secretly expected something really terrific to once again reassure me of the existence of God. I am ashamed that I felt I needed or deserved this confirmation. The quiet and simple way that my faithful mother passed from this temporary life to her permanent place in Heaven was perfect for her and also for me. Undoubtedly, the manner in which my mother lived her life for others was a tribute to God and His overwhelming presence. What more powerful affirmation could I have ever wanted or received?

I think I have finally reached spiritual maturity, perhaps to the point of not needing "signs" from God. I admire people with true faith who don't need some spectacular signification of God's presence. They know He is here and see and feel His presence daily through the loving acts of kindness shown by all of us. God has further revealed Himself through the beauty and magnificence of nature, birds, animals, and sea life. Certainly, we need not look too hard to see God all around us.

No one should need any more of a revelation of God's existence than a sperm and an egg being formed into the intricate network of cells, organs, personality, and gifts that become the incredible, one-and-only being of its kind. But, I know God definitely does sometimes show His presence to us in visible ways. Although I am tremendously blessed to have received the revelation of God's presence many times, even more blessed are those who have not had these signs and still have faith in God.

I guess if I had been a disciple, I unfortunately might have been Thomas, the doubting one. Therefore, special blessings belong to all who have relied on faith alone.

John 20:29:
Jesus then said to him: "You became a believer because
    you saw me.
Blest are they who have not seen and have believed."

I often make birthday cards for family and friends with "30" or "50," or in this case, "86" reasons why I love you to be given to them on their special day. I believe in telling people what they mean to you when they are alive. Not long ago, I found this little card I had created for my mom last year, the year before she died. It pretty much sums up the life she lived and why I was so blessed to have her as my mother.

86 Reasons Why I Love You!

1. You are the best, most loving mother in the world!
2. You are my best friend.
3. You are the most generous person I have ever known!
4. I can always count on you.
5. You are always supportive.
6. You are always positive.
7. You LOVE to shop!
8. You are the best "bargain hunter" shopper.
9. You make the best fresh, cranberry Jello salad on holidays.
10. You took a quiet walk up to Main Street with me in the gentle falling snow at night under the peaceful glow of the streetlight. This remains one of my favorite childhood memories.
11. You used to make us Rice Krispie treats on a Monday night when Gunsmoke was on T.V.
12. You were an excellent seamstress and could sew beautiful clothes for us.
13. You made the bridesmaid dresses for all four of our weddings.
14. You canned every summer using Ball jars and a pressure cooker!

15. You took care of your parents for over twenty years when they were elderly and always exhibited love, patience, and compassion.

16. You married a handsome star athlete and veteran nicknamed Friday.

17. I could tell you anything, even when I was a teenager.

18. You woke me up when I was a child to your melodic voice calling "Good Morning Glory!"

19. You love Esther Price candy!

20. You went to New York with me our first time.

21. You took us by train to Disneyland and Knott's Berry Farm in California when we were kids.

22. You taught me to plant a garden.

23. You slept with me and took care of me in Florida when I was so sick with the baby I miscarried.

24. You babysat my kids when I worked and played Monopoly and read to them for hours.

25. You rode a sled down the basement steps with my kids, like a luge in the Olympics, when you were seventy!

26. You are fun and upbeat.

27. You gave me three amazing sisters – my best friends!

28. You went to Mass with me nearly every day for five years to pray for Patty.

29. You showed the most unconditional love and motherly care standing by Patty throughout her five-year illness with breast cancer.

30. You are one tough cookie.

31. You stay positive despite any circumstances.

32. You taught me how to snap green beans.

33. You let me dress up in a clown suit and sell Kool Aid on Main Street when I was a kid. Oh, my heavens!

34. You let me drag refrigerator boxes home from stores downtown and set up a house made of boxes in our front yard.

35. You made brown Easter eggs with a natural dye from onion skins. I thought they were ugly when I was a kid and only wanted the pretty pastel colored eggs. I never knew how special they were!

36. You had many great friends and taught us how to be a good friend.

37. You always help with my yearly garage sales.

38. We experienced St. Louis together, and you went up in the arch. I did not because I was afraid. You are never afraid.

39. We took our first of many trips to Chicago together in 1982: Garrett's Caramel Corn, Cheesecake Factory under the John Hancock, Christmas windows at Marshall Fields, etc.

40. You are moral.

41. You are faith-filled and taught me to always have faith and never give up.

42. You make a great pot roast and the best pies ever! Sugar cream, black raspberry, and pecan – yum!

43. You let me smash white bread and cut out circles with a metal tea-ball utensil for pretend Holy Communion wafers and put them in a lead crystal dish for a chalice.

44. You put our Christmas packages from Santa on the front porch, while Dad took us for a car ride.
45. You searched everywhere to find my beloved Zippy the Monkey that I wanted for Christmas!
46. You clothed four daughters with fabulous wardrobes.
47. You kept your sanity and patience with four daughters and four monthly cases of PMS!
48. I shared my deepest secrets and my biggest dreams with you.
49. You let Alyssa put make-up on you when she was little, even though you looked like a hooker with bright blue eye shadow, red cheeks and lips and teased-out hair!
50. You are sensible.
51. You love my kids and all of your grandchildren so much!
52. You are a great and loving sister to your brothers and sisters-in-law and adore your nieces and nephews. And they adore you!
53. You love Graeter's black raspberry chip ice cream. Your favorite!
54. You love nuts! Almonds! Cashews! Pecans!
55. You are funny.
56. You went to see The Chipppendales with your twenty-something daughters!
57. You put our hair in "crimpers."
58. The Easter Bunny brought us Esther Price candy.
59. You can tell your original story of "Horace, My Pet Mountain Lion" with your tongue in your cheek.

60. You can make a mouse out of a white handkerchief and make it jump!
61. You (and Dad) took us on a train to California,
62. You (and Dad) took us to Lake Erie with a camper.
63. You knew how to cut bangs too short! Ha!
64. You gave us just the right amount of freedom as teenagers.
65. You have impeccable taste in clothes and furniture.
66. You can always be counted on.
67. You are the most wonderful grandmother.
68. You wear stylish Coach shoes over comfortable shoes.
69. You have a deep devotion to The Blessed Virgin.
70. You pray the rosary every day, just like your mother.
71. You called your father "Daddy."
72. You went to work at Sears to pay for your four daughters' multitude of clothes.
73. You taught us to be kind to everyone and to treat everyone the same.
74. You are not prejudiced.
75. You live a life of truly loving others. I call you "Mother Teresa"- the-second for a reason.
76. You always put others' needs before your own.
77. You cared for many sick and aged persons, expecting and receiving nothing in return.
78. You are beautiful!
79. You made Spritz cookies with a cookie press.
80. You are very intelligent.
81. You are always competent.
82. You have a great sense of humor.

83. You have had a bridge club for 50 years and are an excellent card player.
84. You can eat a whole box of chocolate candy!
85. You made Million Dollar fudge and put it in the green-jeweled fudge dish for Christmas.
86. YOU ARE ABSOLUTELY THE BEST MOTHER IN THE WORLD, AND I AM SO LUCKY TO HAVE YOU!

HAPPY 86th BIRTHDAY, MOTHER!

Love you always,
Beane

My card makes it sound as if Mom's life was all fun and games and happiness. Her life was not easy though. She lived through many challenges and sorrows. Surviving the Depression and enduring the fear and heartache of having her brother in Germany during World War II were exceedingly difficult. She said her heart sank every time she saw a strange car on the street in front of their home, afraid it was a messenger bearing bad news. She always ran home in a panic! Since there were no cell phones or email messages in the forties, everyone waited for months at a time to receive a letter with updates on a loved one's wellbeing.

After giving birth to her fifth daughter, Mom's beautiful, dark-haired, newborn baby girl died in the hospital. I remember when, as a seven-year-old, my dad came home from the hospital and told me our little sister had died. Frantically, I ran into the formal living room and knelt down with my head buried on the sofa, praying for forgiveness through my sobs. I felt so guilty, certain that I had caused my baby sister's death because I had wished for a little brother.

How difficult it must have been to view a baby in a casket and bury an infant child. My parents did not allow me or my sisters to attend the viewing or services. Dad actually seemed to grieve more deeply than Mother. He often talked about little Mary and drove to the cemetery to visit her grave frequently. It was always very evident how much he loved his daughters, so I can only imagine how hard and heartbreaking this loss was for him. Years later, when I lost my own child through a miscarriage, I asked Mother how she was able to handle that tremendous loss. She said that she had four other daughters to care for, so she just had to dive right back into her busy life. Gardening, canning, cooking, cleaning, ironing, sewing, and keeping track of four young girls did indeed keep her busy.

My father suffered a stroke when Mom was just fifty-one years old, and she spent three exceedingly difficult and stressful years caring for him. Every day we drove an hour and a half to the hospital in Dayton to be with Dad. This routine lasted for months. Making matters worse, the great blizzard of 1978 happened during this time, forcing us often to drive on highways that looked like tunnels, with snow piled eight feet high on either side of the road.

My father was admitted to the hospital with life-threatening illnesses many times during the three years following his stroke. On one of those occasions, I was in the middle of a permanent, seeking that big, bold, ultra curly 80's hairstyle at my favorite salon. With soaking wet hair, I rushed to the hospital. Because it was summer and the air-conditioning in the hospital was so cold, I shivered all night long with that wet head. Often, we had to don masks and gowns when visiting Dad because he was placed in isolation due to blood poisoning or some other infection. Priests met us at the hospital six times in one year to give my dad the last rites.

Eventually, my dad had to reside in a nursing home for skilled care. During this period, Dad remained in a debilitating state, being tube fed after suffering an allergic drug reaction. Unable to speak with a "trach tube," he pitifully looked at me with his stunning blue eyes, alerting me that he was trapped in his own body. I went to the nursing home every day to see my dad and then came home and flung myself on my bed, sobbing after almost every visit.

On one particular visit, I witnessed a very poignant and touching moment that I will never forget. Standing just outside the door to Dad's room, I saw Ned Temple, our neighbor and Dad's friend, holding my father's hand and stroking his face while offering soothing words of reassurance. Seeing these two handsome, macho men engaged in a moving and tender expression of friendship was indeed gratifying. I always loved Ned and his wife Jan, but, after that display of affection, I put Ned on a pedestal for the rest of my life.

My father, who died three years after his stroke, was the first person I watched die. I was alone with him in his hospital room when he started to gasp. Hurriedly, I ran to get my sisters in the waiting area so that they could be with him too. Fittingly, the instant that Dad passed, the view of the wintry, gray sky through the large windows revealed the gloomy, dark clouds parting for a glorious sun. Dad had made his quiet passage into Heaven.

I loved and missed my father so much that I hyperventilated after his funeral. I did not accept his death easily. Not unexpectedly, my dad's death was the first of many family losses I would endure. I now find much comfort when I think of all of the wonderful memories with my dad. I was so blessed to have such an amazing father and role model. I smile at the way I eventually followed the examples set by my parents. My father, a convert to Catholicism, always kept a rosary hanging around the knobs of his car radio. When we were teenagers, we would routinely and irreverently yank off the crystal beads so that we could blast our favorite rock music while cruising with our friends. Nevertheless, Dad's dedication became meaningful to me later in life, as I carried on my family's devotion to Mary and our generational tradition of praying the rosary. I still treasure the vivid memory of my grandmother sitting in her chair by the big picture window as she prayed her daily rosary.

In fact, since Mother also recited the rosary daily, this prayer ritual was part of our lives wherever we went. Mom and I were once treated to a trip at the five-star Ritz Carlton in New Orleans by my sister Kathy. We experienced a very turbulent flight on the way to Louisiana, as our seats were in the last row right above the engine. I felt so sick and dizzy throughout the air travel that my head was literally spinning. It was dreadful!

Needless to say, on the way home I boarded the plane, and there it was! My seat was the only one left in the last row again. That seat! The agitator seat! I became overwhelmed with anxiety, certain I could not endure a flight like that again. I just wanted to escape from the nearest exit and take up permanent residence in New Orleans. I quietly asked the flight attendant if I could possibly be assigned another seat.

She loudly announced to the entire plane, "We have a fearful flyer here! Anybody want to change seats?"

I could have died! I might as well have been browsing in a drug store, where an anonymous employee announced over an intercom, "Would an associate please help the tall brunette in aisle three find the Preparation H!" I was so humiliated!

Mercifully, a good-hearted businessman kindly offered to exchange seats. I thanked him profusely and meekly slid down into the security of my new seat.

The flight attendant sensed my embarrassment and whispered, "It's alright, honey, some lady in the back row is praying a rosary!"

I glanced up at her and opened my clenched fist, exposing my own rosary.

"That's my mother!" I quietly admitted, as I rolled my eyes toward the back of the plane.

So, it is readily apparent that the rosary is an integral part of our lives, with the focus always on the life of Jesus. The rosary is a protective veil and also a way we can get closer to Jesus through His mother. Therefore, I pray to Mary, asking for her intercession in the way I would approach my own earthly mother to be of assistance. My sister, Marie, believes a woman can never have too many pairs of shoes. Similarly, I have dozens of rosaries that have been given to me as gifts or that I have inherited from relatives. I must believe that one can never have too many rosaries!

I am sure my mother's daily prayers gave her the fortitude that she needed to endure all of life's struggles. She spent over twenty years caring for her aging parents instead of sending them to a nursing home. This responsibility included feeding, bathing, diapering, and tending to all of their needs. Out of necessity, Mom was often up through the night, and in the years that followed, she slept little. I learned my future role as a caregiver from the best teacher in the world.

"Love You Forever" is one of my favorite books. When I read that book to my children, I reminisced about my own mother caring for her parents and the role reversal of parent and child. I thought about Mom holding her mother's aged and shriveled body in her arms and spoon-feeding her. Her mother died at age ninety-three and her father died at one-hundred and one. Even though Mom sacrificed so much for both of her parents, she never complained. Her unwavering example taught us love, compassion, and endurance. Most of all, she taught us to honor your father and your mother. Mom truly saw the face of God in her parents. Mother Teresa said, "Do you want to do something beautiful for God? There is a person who needs you. This is your chance." We can all do something beautiful for God.

While recently watching the NBC evening news highlighting the Pope's visit to orphaned children in Manila, my eyes welled with tears of empathy. I commented to my husband how deeply I respected Pope Francis and the beautiful pastoral ministry he performs for God.

"He is truly a saint!" I proclaimed, revealing my awe and admiration for this incredible man.

"Marlene, your own mother was truly a saint! I have never met anyone like her!" Steve responded.

What a wonderful statement for Steve to make about his mother-in-law. I was deeply touched by this glowing compliment. To emphasize his point, Steve began repeating all of her selfless, kind, and generous actions. He recalled how she had always put others before herself for all of the forty-five years that he had known her. Besides caring for my ailing father and her aging parents, Mom also babysat my two children while I worked, creating many endearing lifetime memories with her grandchildren. Watching her nieces and nephews was another welcomed task which was very enjoyable for my mother. Mom was always willing to lend a hand to anyone in need, especially someone less fortunate. She spent years caring for three elderly ladies. This responsibility entailed spending time away from her own immediate family while she took care of people who had no one else. She chauffeured them to appointments, sat for hours in emergency and hospital rooms, and stayed overnight with them when necessary. Most of her good deeds were performed without any compensation. The joy that came from helping others was enough reward for her. Of course, like all humans, Mom was not perfect. She may have uttered a curse word occasionally or revealed some other human weaknesses, but, to me, Mother definitely was a living saint.

There are many saints living among us in this world, even though they may not be canonized and are not celebrated with a feast day. These special people, however, can be remembered and celebrated by the family members and friends who love them. Grace Ballinger, Virginia Bryan, Dorothy Hoyng, Diane Menchhofer, Jane Schelich, and Ruth Weidman are friends of mine for whom I have very deep admiration. These women, as well as many other saintly mothers and fathers I know, have dedicated their entire lives to the total care of their children, who were disabled from accidents, illnesses, or birth defects. Their selflessness inspires countless others to be more compassionate human beings. Most assuredly, these saints will be acknowledged by God and will enjoy an everlasting feast day.

When my youngest sister died following an anguishing five-year battle with breast cancer, Mother faced her deepest challenge and sorrow. It was definitely the hardest and most heartbreaking five years of my own life and my family's as well. To watch someone you love, especially a child, suffer so tremendously must be the most painful trial that life presents.

Mother was there for her daughter every step of the way. She prayed continually and never lost her faith even though it was certainly challenged many times. I know Mom never overcame the loss of her beloved Patty. There were times when she was angry at God and wondered how He could ever have allowed this tragedy to happen. God never wills bad things to happen to one of His children. It was all very hard for Mother to understand, but she still went to Mass and prayed continually. I cannot comprehend how devastating it is for a parent to bury a child. When I suffered my miscarriage, I often prayed to God that He would never let me lose another child. Mother was extremely close to Patty, and it is so fitting that she is now with her in Heaven for eternity.

My mom faced many more challenges in life, but I have recounted her most difficult struggles. Her own illness with leukemia proved her strong character and a mother's ever-present protection of her children. Mom's strength and fortitude were both remarkable and inspiring. She was always positive and upbeat despite any circumstances.

I surely do miss my mother popping in my house, although sometimes those unannounced visits happened at an inopportune or comical time. My daughter went through a phase as a preteen during which she liked that instant noodle soup that comes packaged in an envelope. She decided to make a bowl one day after we had spent an afternoon at the swimming pool. I gave her the nickname "The Spill Queen" for a reason. No sooner had Alyssa carried the soup into the family room and deposited on the coffee table than it spilled on the beige carpet. I was on my hands and knees in a skimpy swimsuit trying to scrub the fluorescent yellow stain from my carpet. At the same time, I was scolding Alyssa with some very choice words. Suddenly, I looked up and saw a priest from India standing in my doorway! My behavior was so bad that I initially wondered when priests started making house calls for confession! Evidently, a relative had paid for his education, and my mother chose this awkward moment to bring him over to meet me. What a great first impression I must have made!

I would love to have my mother pop into my house again, even just one more time. I wouldn't care at all if she brought an unannounced guest and caught me in another embarrassing moment. And it would be wonderful to have the chance to go shopping with her again. She had the most excellent taste and always found amazing designer clothing at an incredible sale price. Struggling with debilitating weakness less than two weeks before she died, Mother still insisted on going shopping with me to Ft. Wayne to find a dress to wear to The Harvard Club in New York City to meet Fred Sievert, former President of New York Life and author of God Revealed. Unfortunately, my mom's health deteriorated so rapidly that I did not make it to New York. It seemed fitting that I wore the new black dress we bought on our last shopping trip together to her funeral.

I surely miss Mom eating dinner with us nearly every evening. I miss her help, support, and advice tremendously! We always need our mothers, no matter how old we are. It is so important for us to cherish every precious moment with our mothers, and all of our loved ones, for as long as they are here with us.

I dream of reuniting with my mother, father, sisters, grandparents, in-laws, and friends in Heaven someday. The way I like to talk, it will take an eternity for me to catch up with everyone! Heaven Came to Me but one day I want to hear God say, "Come to Heaven, Marlene!"

Acknowledgments

I have been encouraged by many people to write my story to inspire others and to instill a faith in God. My hope is that many people will see how God has been present in their own lives as well.

I want to extend my inexpressible gratitude to my beloved Father Angelo Caserta for his prayers, spiritual guidance, support, and love as I have undertaken this personal journey. Father Caserta's blessing was the deciding factor in publishing Heaven Came to Me. I knew going forward was the right decision because of his encouragement.

I also cannot adequately thank my longtime friend and gifted national speaker, Father Andrew O'Reilly, for his words of encouragement and positive reinforcement. Father Andy truly believed in my book as being worthy of his support.

Two exceptional people that deserve a sincere thank you for additional spiritual guidance are Sharon Showman, M.Div., Ph.D., Assistant Professor of Communication and Religion, Wright State University-Lake Campus, and, Claudia Coe, a certified life coach. Claudia coaches at the U.S. Naval Academy and is Director of Community Service Initiatives for the Annapolis Leadership Center. I am so grateful to these very special friends.

Special thanks are due to my husband, Steve, my children, and my family for their assistance and love. Steve gave me the courage to proceed with this project every step of the way.

I want to extend my heartfelt thanks to Mr. Fred Sievert, author of God Revealed and former President of New York Life, for publishing several of my stories on his website. The many comments I received stating the impact my experiences made on the lives of readers were the impetus for this publication.

My life was profoundly impacted when I met Susan Conroy, author of "Mother Teresa's Lessons of Love & Secrets of Sanctity." I want to express my sincere gratitude to Susan because I was so deeply inspired by her work alongside Mother Teresa in India and the life changing lessons that she taught me through her book.

Most importantly, I would like to express my deepest thanks to Tom Watts, a retired English teacher and friend, who was kind enough to assist me with the meticulous editing of my work.

About the Author

Marlene Sommer's personal experience of losing five family members to cancer has instilled a passion to help others fighting this devastating disease. She has been privileged to serve as two-term President and board member of The Cancer Association of Mercer County (facebook page: Cancer Association of Mercer County). This amazing organization has given over a million dollars in financial aid to cancer patients in her county. In 2007 her sister Patrice Menchhofer inspired her to give women who are undergoing cancer treatment a pleasurable and relaxing respite. The idea grew with the support of the Cancer Association of Mercer County and many other amazing people in her community. Last year approximately one-hundred women attended the 8th "Patty's Night Out," where they enjoyed free manicures, skin care, make-up, hair styles, massages, yoga, music, delicious food, flowers, and lovely gifts all donated by local businesses, restaurants, and organizations. A Men's Night Out was also started four years ago for a meal, entertainment, and gifts for male cancer survivors. Patrice's Place (facebook page) is a non-profit organization inspired by her sister, Patrice, and founded in 2007 by Marlene, with a goal of raising awareness and providing comfort, relaxation, and spiritual guidance for people coping with cancer. One-hundred percent of Marlene's profits from her "Stick Your Neck Out" to end cancer T-shirts, featuring flamingos and giraffes, are used to give physical, emotional, spiritual, and financial support to anyone with the diagnosis of cancer.

She would like to use profits from her T-shirts and books to start non-profit respite centers for cancer patients called "A Summer Place." Each location of "A Summer Place" would be dedicated to someone, with the first one to be designated, "Patrice's Place," in honor of her sister. Other locations could be started and dedicated to survivors, including celebrity survivors, all over the country. In the summer of 2006, after two years of watching her sister suffering with cancer, her family spent a week with Patrice on the beach in South Carolina. Marlene and Patrice were reclining in hammocks, looking up at a gorgeous blue sky with a plethora of palm trees towering above their sand-kissed toes, while pelicans flew effortlessly overhead, and the soothing sound of the ocean waves relaxed them completely. The two sisters sipped fresh squeezed lemonade with crushed strawberries, oblivious to all of their worries for a fleeting moment. Enjoying life for the first time in so long, Marlene concluded that this refuge is what every person who is going through cancer treatment deserves!

Marlene wants a place where cancer patients can go to escape cancer for an hour or an afternoon and enjoy the pleasure of a summer day. She wants them to feel sand squishing between their toes and to relax in a hammock, enjoying a healthful smoothie, and imagining that they are at the ocean! Patients often cannot go out of town even for a day during treatment, but they could go to this respite for a massage, a pedicure, a movie, or anything to give a small pleasure.

It is Marlene's hope that God turns all of her dreams into a reality. She often reflects on her favorite quote from Dom Helder Camara, "When we are dreaming alone it is only a dream. When we are dreaming with others, it is the beginning of reality."

CPSIA information can be obtained at www.ICGtesting.com
Printed in the USA
BVOW02s1529041115

425713BV00005B/76/P